A narrative of the mutiny, on board His Majesty's ship Bounty; and the subsequent voyage of part of the crew, ... Written by Lieutenant William Bligh. ...

William Bligh

ECCO
PRINT EDITIONS

A narrative of the mutiny, on board His Majesty's ship Bounty; and the subsequent voyage of part of the crew, ... Written by Lieutenant William Bligh. ...
Bligh, William
ESTCID: T007185
Reproduction from British Library
Later incorporated, in an adapted version, in 'A voyage to the South Sea', 1792.
London : printed for George Nicol, 1790.
iv,88p.,plates : maps ; 4°

Eighteenth Century
Collections Online
Print Editions

Gale ECCO Print Editions

Relive history with *Eighteenth Century Collections Online,* now available in print for the independent historian and collector. This series includes the most significant English-language and foreign-language works printed in Great Britain during the eighteenth century, and is organized in seven different subject areas including literature and language; medicine, science, and technology; and religion and philosophy. The collection also includes thousands of important works from the Americas.

The eighteenth century has been called "The Age of Enlightenment." It was a period of rapid advance in print culture and publishing, in world exploration, and in the rapid growth of science and technology – all of which had a profound impact on the political and cultural landscape. At the end of the century the American Revolution, French Revolution and Industrial Revolution, perhaps three of the most significant events in modern history, set in motion developments that eventually dominated world political, economic, and social life.

In a groundbreaking effort, Gale initiated a revolution of its own: digitization of epic proportions to preserve these invaluable works in the largest online archive of its kind. Contributions from major world libraries constitute over 175,000 original printed works. Scanned images of the actual pages, rather than transcriptions, recreate the works *as they first appeared.*

Now for the first time, these high-quality digital scans of original works are available via print-on-demand, making them readily accessible to libraries, students, independent scholars, and readers of all ages.

For our initial release we have created seven robust collections to form one the world's most comprehensive catalogs of 18th century works.

Initial Gale ECCO Print Editions collections include:

History and Geography
Rich in titles on English life and social history, this collection spans the world as it was known to eighteenth-century historians and explorers. Titles include a wealth of travel accounts and diaries, histories of nations from throughout the world, and maps and charts of a world that was still being discovered. Students of the War of American Independence will find fascinating accounts from the British side of conflict.

Social Science

Delve into what it was like to live during the eighteenth century by reading the first-hand accounts of everyday people, including city dwellers and farmers, businessmen and bankers, artisans and merchants, artists and their patrons, politicians and their constituents. Original texts make the American, French, and Industrial revolutions vividly contemporary.

Medicine, Science and Technology

Medical theory and practice of the 1700s developed rapidly, as is evidenced by the extensive collection, which includes descriptions of diseases, their conditions, and treatments. Books on science and technology, agriculture, military technology, natural philosophy, even cookbooks, are all contained here.

Literature and Language

Western literary study flows out of eighteenth-century works by Alexander Pope, Daniel Defoe, Henry Fielding, Frances Burney, Denis Diderot, Johann Gottfried Herder, Johann Wolfgang von Goethe, and others. Experience the birth of the modern novel, or compare the development of language using dictionaries and grammar discourses.

Religion and Philosophy

The Age of Enlightenment profoundly enriched religious and philosophical understanding and continues to influence present-day thinking. Works collected here include masterpieces by David Hume, Immanuel Kant, and Jean-Jacques Rousseau, as well as religious sermons and moral debates on the issues of the day, such as the slave trade. The Age of Reason saw conflict between Protestantism and Catholicism transformed into one between faith and logic -- a debate that continues in the twenty-first century.

Law and Reference

This collection reveals the history of English common law and Empire law in a vastly changing world of British expansion. Dominating the legal field is the *Commentaries of the Law of England* by Sir William Blackstone, which first appeared in 1765. Reference works such as almanacs and catalogues continue to educate us by revealing the day-to-day workings of society.

Fine Arts

The eighteenth-century fascination with Greek and Roman antiquity followed the systematic excavation of the ruins at Pompeii and Herculaneum in southern Italy; and after 1750 a neoclassical style dominated all artistic fields. The titles here trace developments in mostly English-language works on painting, sculpture, architecture, music, theater, and other disciplines. Instructional works on musical instruments, catalogs of art objects, comic operas, and more are also included.

The BiblioLife Network

This project was made possible in part by the BiblioLife Network (BLN), a project aimed at addressing some of the huge challenges facing book preservationists around the world. The BLN includes libraries, library networks, archives, subject matter experts, online communities and library service providers. We believe every book ever published should be available as a high-quality print reproduction; printed on-demand anywhere in the world. This insures the ongoing accessibility of the content and helps generate sustainable revenue for the libraries and organizations that work to preserve these important materials.

The following book is in the "public domain" and represents an authentic reproduction of the text as printed by the original publisher. While we have attempted to accurately maintain the integrity of the original work, there are sometimes problems with the original work or the micro-film from which the books were digitized. This can result in minor errors in reproduction. Possible imperfections include missing and blurred pages, poor pictures, markings and other reproduction issues beyond our control. Because this work is culturally important, we have made it available as part of our commitment to protecting, preserving, and promoting the world's literature.

GUIDE TO FOLD-OUTS MAPS and OVERSIZED IMAGES

The book you are reading was digitized from microfilm captured over the past thirty to forty years. Years after the creation of the original microfilm, the book was converted to digital files and made available in an online database.

In an online database, page images do not need to conform to the size restrictions found in a printed book. When converting these images back into a printed bound book, the page sizes are standardized in ways that maintain the detail of the original. For large images, such as fold-out maps, the original page image is split into two or more pages

Guidelines used to determine how to split the page image follows:

• Some images are split vertically; large images require vertical and horizontal splits.
• For horizontal splits, the content is split left to right.
• For vertical splits, the content is split from top to bottom.
• For both vertical and horizontal splits, the image is processed from top left to bottom right.

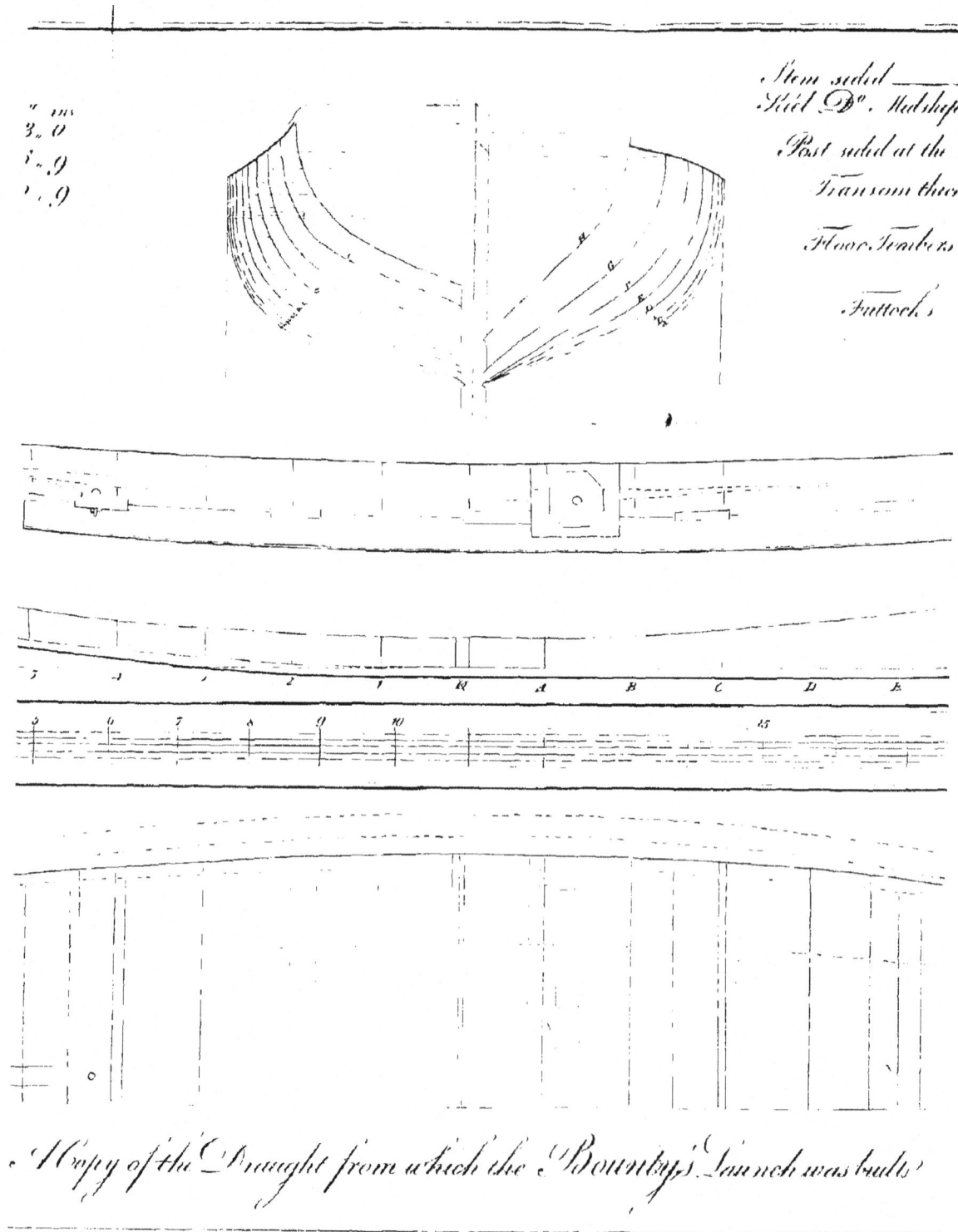

A Copy of the Draught from which the Bounty's Launch was built

		Ft	ins
		0,	3½
		0,	3⅞
{ Tuck		0,	3½
{ . Alow		0,	3
{		0,	2
{ Sided		0,	2
{ . Moulded at the Heads		0,	2⅓
{ Throat		0,	3⅞
{ Sided Alow		0,	2
{ Square at the Heads		0,	1⅞

A

NARRATIVE

OF THE

MUTINY,

ON BOARD

HIS MAJESTY's SHIP *BOUNTY*;

AND THE

SUBSEQUENT VOYAGE OF PART OF THE CREW,

IN THE SHIP's BOAT,

From Tofoa, one of the Friendly Iflands,

To Timor, a Dutch Settlement in the Eaft Indies.

———————————————

Written by Lieutenant WILLIAM BLIGH.

———————————————

ILLUSTRATED WITH CHARTS

———————————————

LONDON·

PRINTED FOR GEORGE NICOL, BOOKSELLER TO HIS MAJESTY, PALL-MALL.

MDCCXC.

ADVERTISEMENT.

THE following Narrative is only a part of a voyage undertaken for the purpofe of conveying the Bread-fruit Tree from the South Sea Iflands to the Weft Indies. The manner in which this expedition mifcarried, with the fubfequent tranfactions and events, are here related. This part of the voyage is not firft in the order of time, yet the circumftances are fo diftinct from that by which it was preceded, that it appears unneceffary to delay giving as much early information as poffible concerning fo extraordinary an event. The reft will be laid before the Public as foon as it can be got ready; and it is intended to publifh it in fuch a manner, as, with the prefent Narrative, will make the account of the voyage compleat.

At prefent, for the better underftanding the following pages, it is fufficient to inform the reader, that in

Auguft,

Auguſt, 1787, I was appointed to command the Bounty, a ſhip of 215 tons burthen, carrying 4 ſix-pounders, 4 ſwivels, and 46 men, including myſelf and every perſon on board. We ſailed from England in December, 1787, and arrived at Otaheite the 26th of October, 1788. On the 4th of April, 1789, we left Otaheite, with every favourable appearance of completing the object of the voyage, in a manner equal to my moſt ſanguine expectations. At this period the enſuing Narrative commences.

NARRATIVE,

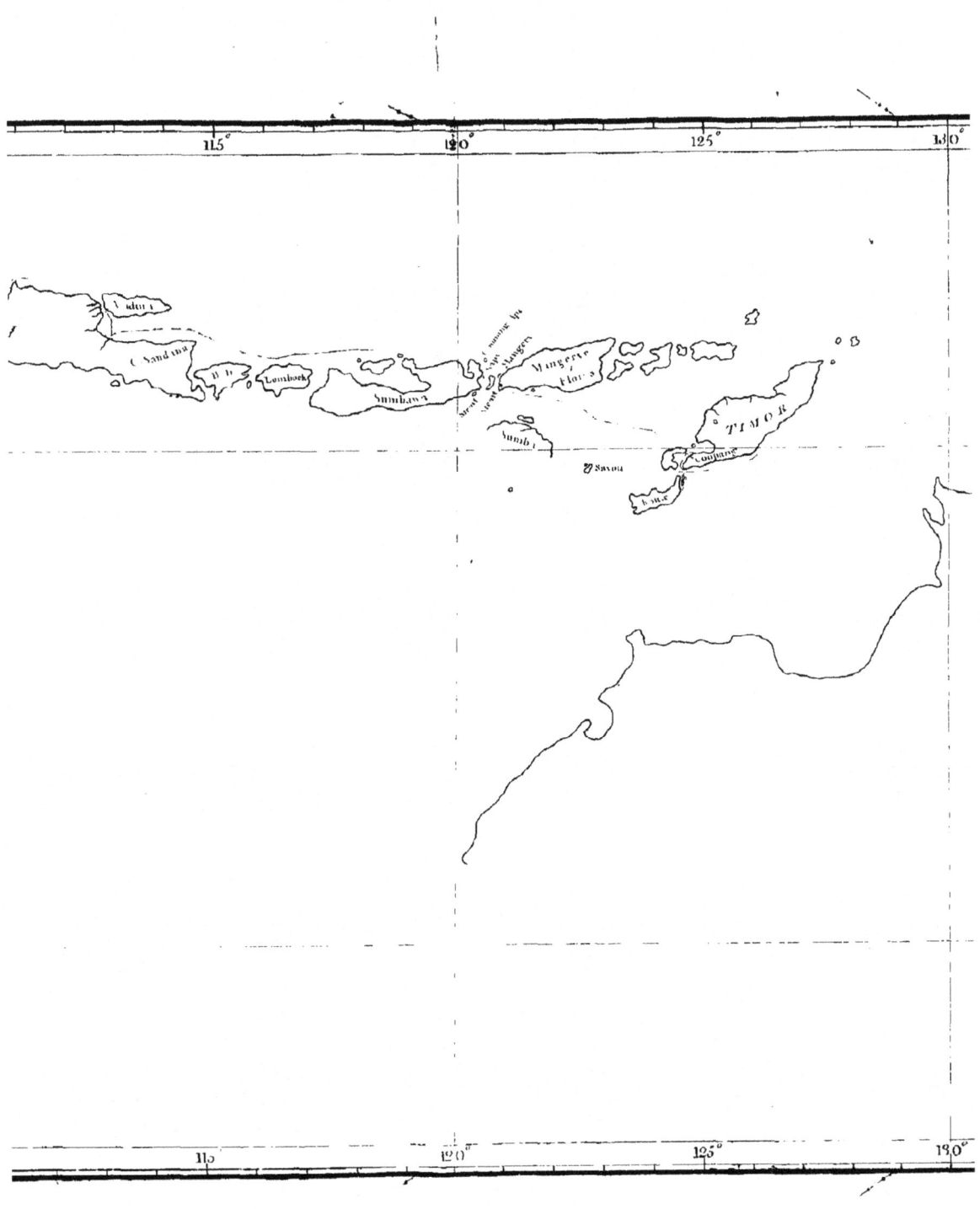

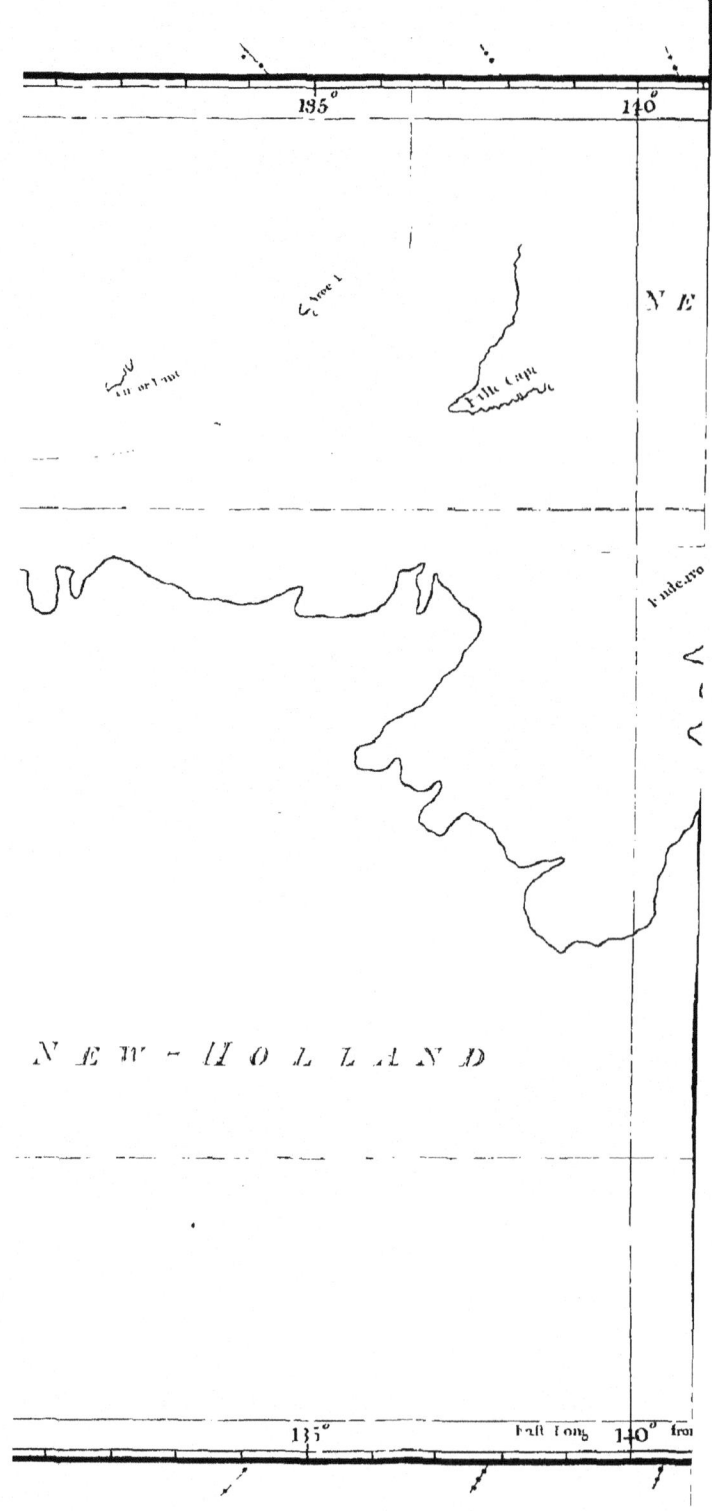

135° 140°

N E

N E W - H O L L A N D

135° East Long 140° from

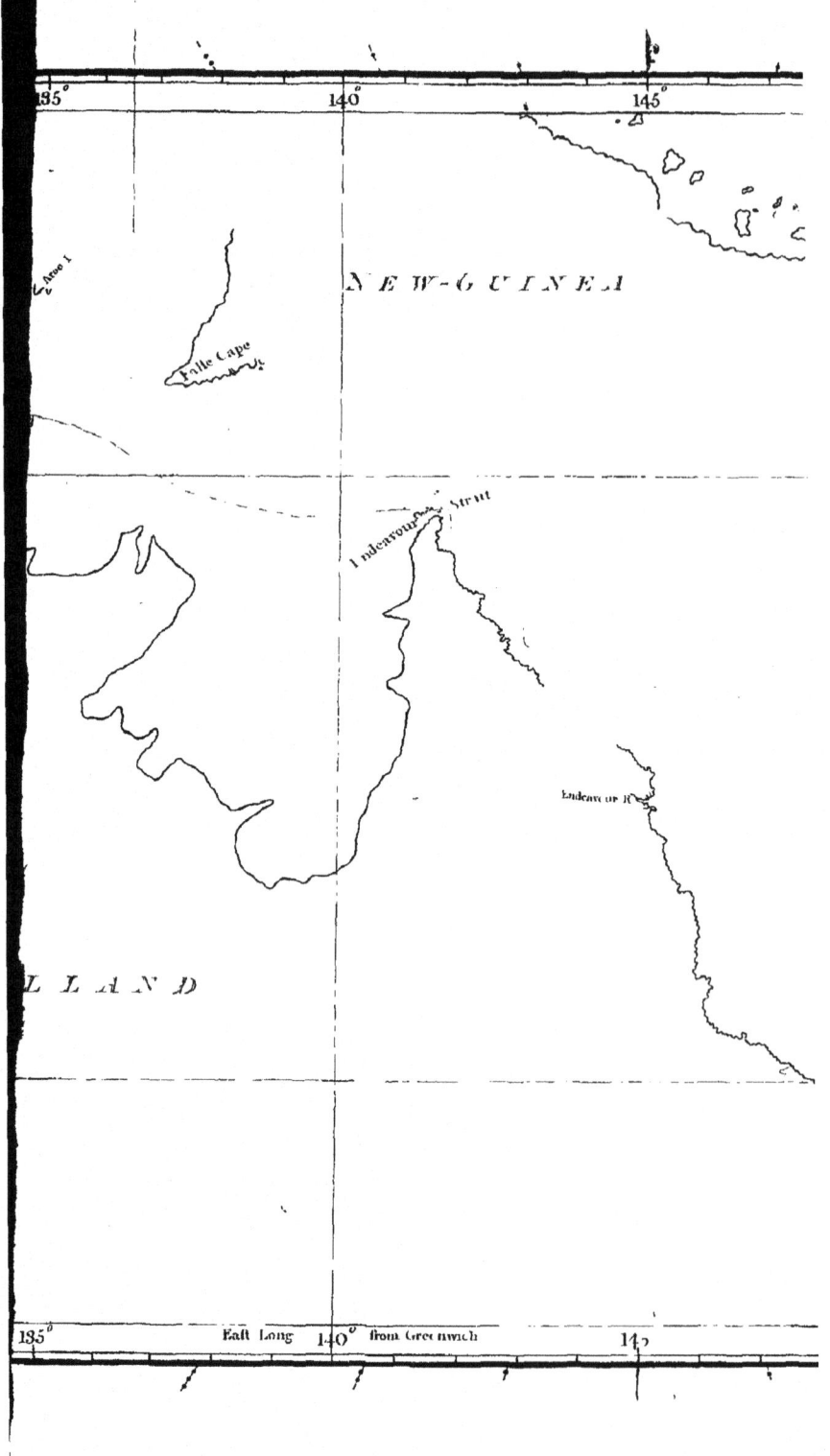

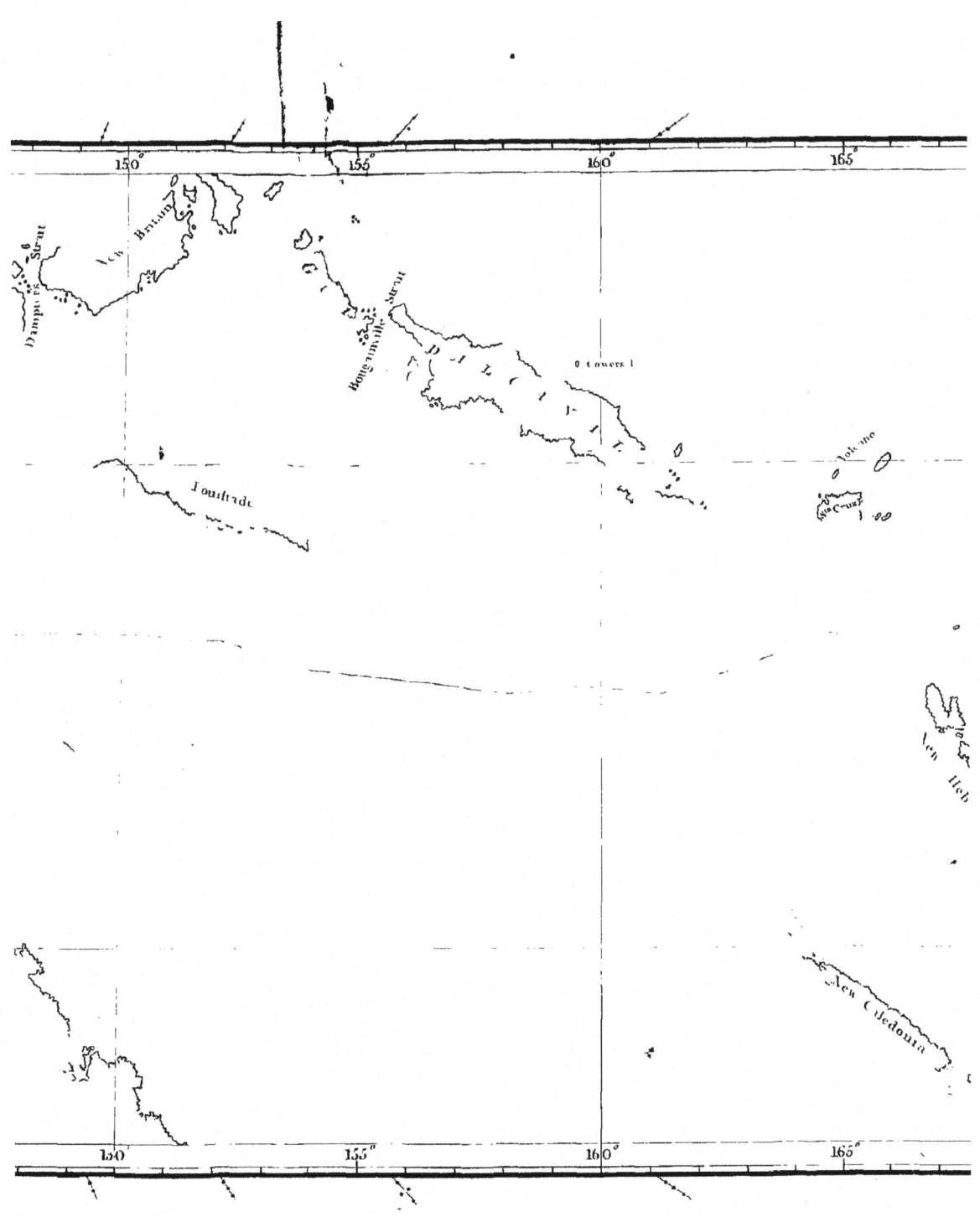

170°   175°   180°

170°   175°   180°

Bligh's Islands

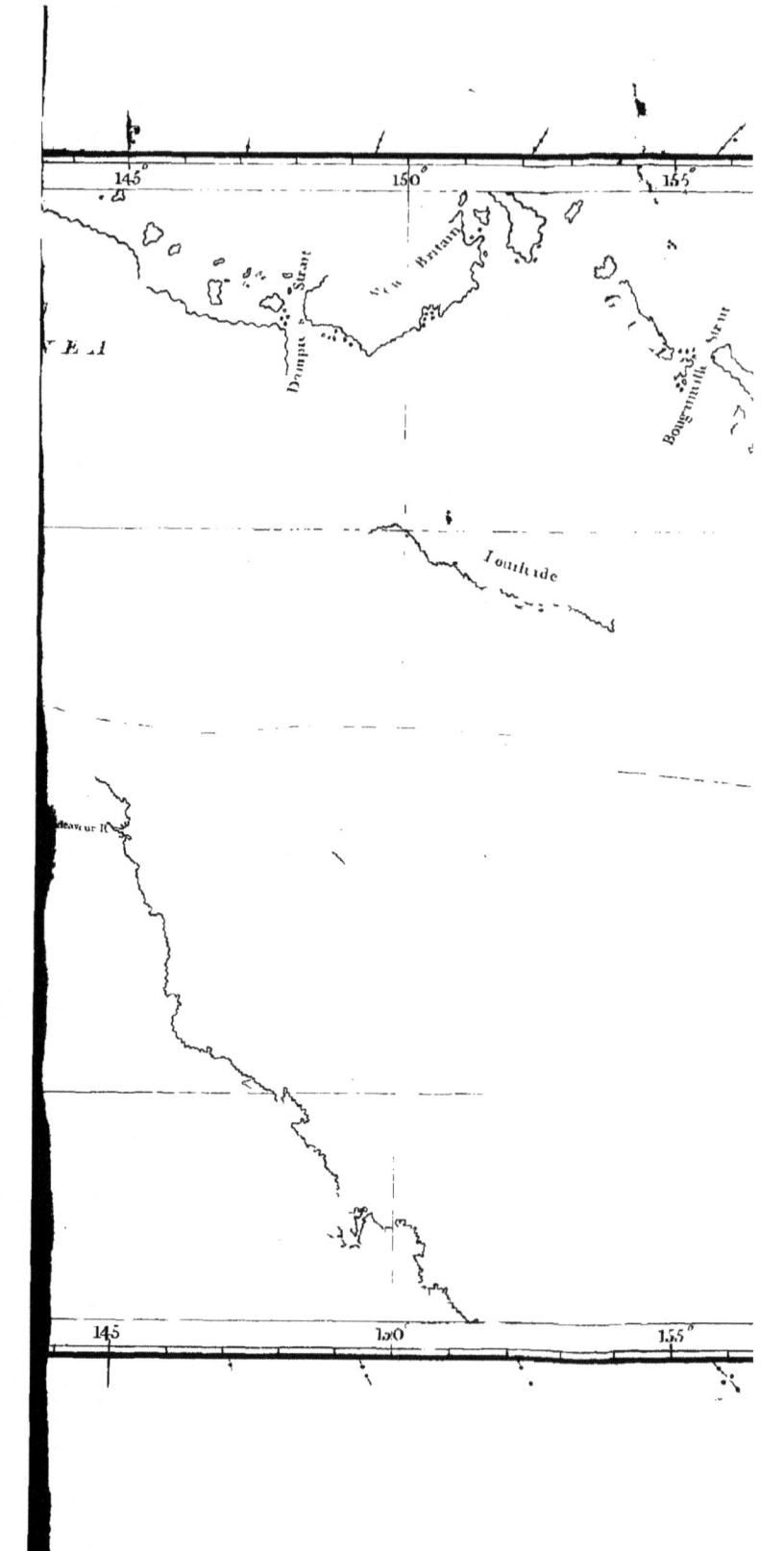

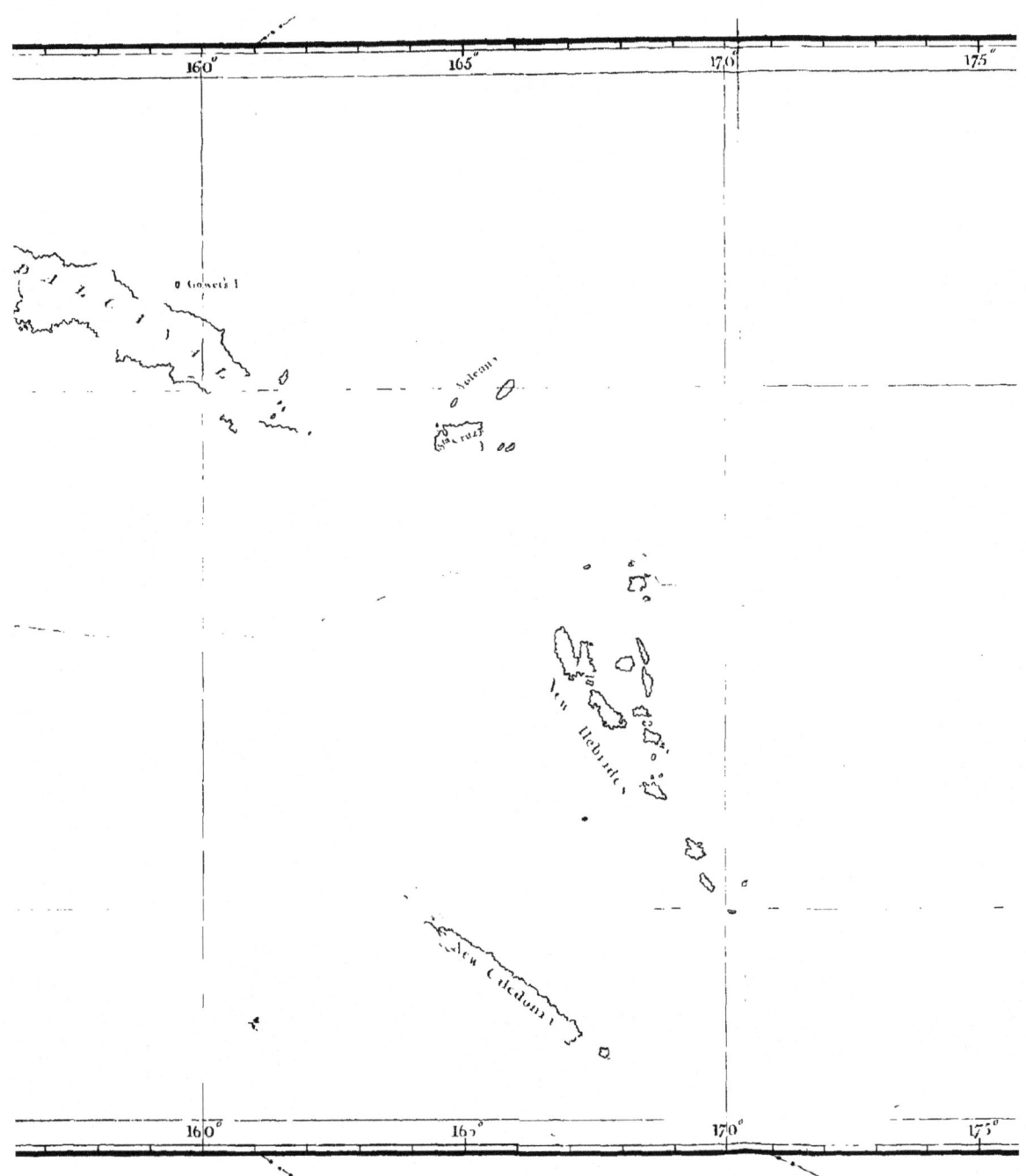

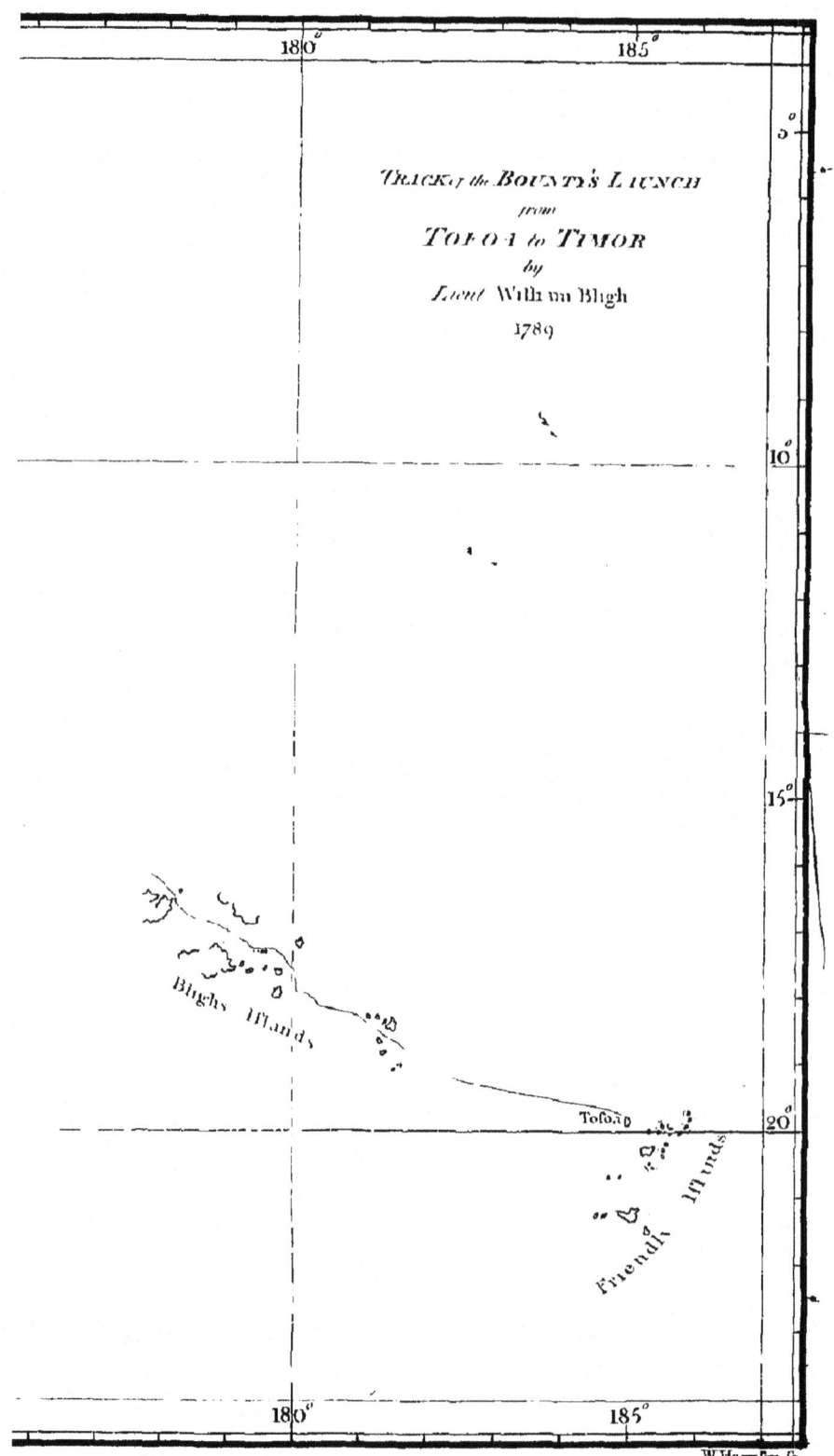

TRACK of the BOUNTY'S LAUNCH
from
TOFOA to TIMOR
by
Lieut William Bligh
1789

180°   185°

5°

10°

15°

Bligh's Islands

Tofoa   20°

Friendly Islands

180°   185°

W. Harrison sc

A
N A R R A T I V E, &c.

I SAILED from Otaheite on the 4th of April 1789, having on board 1015 fine bread-fruit plants, befides many other valuable fruits of that country, which, with unremitting attention, we had been collecting for three and twenty weeks, and which were now in the higheft ftate of perfection.

On the 11th of April, I difcovered an ifland in latitude 18° 52' S. and longitude 200° 19' E. by the natives called Whytootackee. On the 24th we anchored at Annamooka, one of the Friendly Iflands; from which, after completing our wood and water, I failed on the 27th, having every reafon to expect, from the fine condition of the plants, that they would continue healthy.

On the evening of the 28th, owing to light winds, we were not clear of the iflands, and at night I directed my courfe towards Tofoa. The mafter had the firft watch; the gunner the middle watch; and Mr. Chriftian, one of the mates, the morning watch. This was the turn of duty for the night.

Juft before fun-rifing, Mr. Chriftian, with the mafter at arms, gunner's mate, and Thomas Burket, feaman, came into my cabin while I was afleep, and feizing me, tied my hands with a cord behind my back, and threatened me with inftant death, if I fpoke or made the leaft noife: I,

B however,

1789.
APRIL.

however, called fo loud as to alarm every one; but they had already fecured the officers who were not of their party, by placing centinels at their doors. There were three men at my cabin door, befides the four within; Chriftian had only a cutlafs in his hand, the others had mufkets and bayonets. I was hauled out of bed, and forced on deck in my fhirt, fuffering great pain from the tightnefs with which they had tied my hands. I demanded the reafon of fuch violence, but received no other anfwer than threats of inftant death, if I did not hold my tongue. Mr. Elphinfton, the mafter's mate, was kept in his birth; Mr. Nelfon, botanift, Mr. Peckover, gunner, Mr. Ledward, furgeon, and the mafter, were confined to their cabins; and alfo the clerk, Mr. Samuel, but he foon obtained leave to come on deck. The fore hatchway was guarded by centinels; the boatfwain and carpenter were, however, allowed to come on deck, where they faw me ftanding abaft the mizen-maft, with my hands tied behind my back, under a guard, with Chriftian at their head.

The boatfwain was now ordered to hoift the launch out, with a threat, if he did not do it inftantly, to take care of himfelf.

The boat being out, Mr. Hayward and Mr. Hallet, midfhipmen, and Mr. Samuel, were ordered into it; upon which I demanded the caufe of fuch an order, and endeavoured to perfuade fome one to a fenfe of duty; but it was to no effect: " Hold your tongue, Sir, or you are dead this " inftant," was conftantly repeated to me.

The mafter, by this time, had fent to be allowed to come on deck, which was permitted; but he was foon ordered back again to his cabin.

I continued my endeavours to turn the tide of affairs,
when

when Chriftian changed the cutlafs he had in his hand for a bayonet, that was brought to him, and, holding me with a ftrong gripe by the cord that tied my hands, he with many oaths threatened to kill me immediately if I would not be quiet: the villains round me had their pieces cocked and bayonets fixed. Particular people were now called on to go into the boat, and were hurried over the fide: whence I concluded that with thefe people I was to be fet adrift.

I therefore made another effort to bring about a change, but with no other effect than to be threatened with having my brains blown out.

The boatfwain and feamen, who were to go in the boat, were allowed to collect twine, canvas, lines, fails, cordage, an eight and twenty gallon cafk of water, and the carpenter to take his tool cheft. Mr. Samuel got 150lbs of bread, with a fmall quantity of rum and wine. He alfo got a quadrant and compafs into the boat; but was forbidden, on pain of death, to touch either map, ephemeris, book of aftronomical obfervations, fextant, time-keeper, or any of my furveys or drawings.

The mutineers now hurried thofe they meant to get rid of into the boat. When moft of them were in, Chriftian directed a dram to be ferved to each of his own crew. I now unhappily faw that nothing could be done to effect the recovery of the fhip: there was no one to affift me, and every endeavour on my part was anfwered with threats of death.

The officers were called, and forced over the fide into the boat, while I was kept apart from every one, abaft the mizen-maft; Chriftian, armed with a bayonet, holding me by the bandage that fecured my hands. The

B 2 · guard

guard round me had their pieces cocked, but, on my daring the ungrateful wretches to fire, they uncocked them.

Isaac Martin, one of the guard over me, I saw, had an inclination to assist me, and, as he fed me with shaddock, (my lips being quite parched with my endeavours to bring about a change) we explained our wishes to each other by our looks; but this being observed, Martin was instantly removed from me; his inclination then was to leave the ship, for which purpose he got into the boat; but with many threats they obliged him to return.

The armourer, Joseph Coleman, and the two carpenters, M'Intosh and Norman, were also kept contrary to their inclination; and they begged of me, after I was astern in the boat, to remember that they declared they had no hand in the transaction. Michael Byrne, I am told, likewise wanted to leave the ship.

It is of no moment for me to recount my endeavours to bring back the offenders to a sense of their duty: all I could do was by speaking to them in general; but my endeavours were of no avail, for I was kept securely bound, and no one but the guard suffered to come near me.

To Mr. Samuel I am indebted for securing my journals and commission, with some material ship papers. Without these I had nothing to certify what I had done, and my honour and character might have been suspected, without my possessing a proper document to have defended them. All this he did with great resolution, though guarded and strictly watched. He attempted to save the time-keeper, and a box with all my surveys, drawings, and remarks for fifteen years past, which were numerous; when he was hurried away, with " Damn your eyes, you are well off to " get what you have."

It

It appeared to me, that Chriſtian was ſome time in doubt whether he ſhould keep the carpenter, or his mates; at length he determined on the latter, and the carpenter was ordered into the boat. He was permitted, but not without ſome oppoſition, to take his tool cheſt.

Much altercation took place among the mutinous crew during the whole buſineſs : ſome ſwore " I'll be damned if " he does not find his way home, if he gets any thing with " him," (meaning me); others, when the carpenter's cheſt was carrying away, " Damn my eyes, he will have a veſ- " ſel built in a month." While others laughed at the helpleſs ſituation of the boat, being very deep, and ſo little room for thoſe who were in her. As for Chriſtian, he ſeemed meditating inſtant deſtruction on himſelf and every one.

I aſked for arms, but they laughed at me, and ſaid I was well acquainted with the people where I was going, and therefore did not want them; four cutlaſſes, however, were thrown into the boat, after we were veered aſtern.

When the officers and men, with whom I was ſuffered to have no communication, were put into the boat, they only waited for me, and the maſter at arms informed Chriſtian of it; who then ſaid—" Come, captain Bligh, your officers and " men are now in the boat, and you muſt go with them; if " you attempt to make the leaſt reſiſtance you will inſtantly " be put to death:" and, without any farther ceremony, holding me by the cord that tied my hands, with a tribe of armed ruffians about me, I was forced over the ſide, where they untied my hands. Being in the boat we were veered aſtern by a rope. A few pieces of pork were then thrown to us, and ſome cloaths, alſo the cutlaſſes I have already mentioned; and it was now that the armourer

and

and carpenters called out to me to remember that they had no hand in the transaction. After having undergone a great deal of ridicule, and been kept some time to make sport for these unfeeling wretches, we were at length cast adrift in the open ocean.

I had with me in the boat the following persons:

Names.	Stations.
JOHN FRYER	Master.
THOMAS LEDWARD	Acting Surgeon.
DAVID NELSON	Botanist.
WILLIAM PECKOVER	Gunner.
WILLIAM COLE	Boatswain.
WILLIAM PURCELL	Carpenter.
WILLIAM ELPHINSTON	Master's Mate.
THOMAS HAYWARD	}Midshipmen.
JOHN HALLET	
JOHN NORTON	}Quarter Masters.
PETER LINKLETTER	
LAWRENCE LEBOGUE	Sailmaker.
JOHN SMITH	}Cooks.
THOMAS HALL	
GEORGE SIMPSON	Quarter Master's Mate.
ROBERT TINKLER	A boy.
ROBERT LAMB	Butcher.
Mr. SAMUEL	Clerk.

There remained on board the Bounty, as pirates,

FLETCHER CHRISTIAN	Master's Mate.
PETER HAYWOOD	}Midshipmen.
EDWARD YOUNG	
GEORGE STEWART	

CHARLES

Names.	Stations.
CHARLES CHURCHILL	Master at Arms.
JOHN MILLS	Gunner's Mate.
JAMES MORRISON	Boatswain's Mate.
THOMAS BURKITT	Able Seaman.
MATTHEW QUINTAL	Ditto.
JOHN SUMNER	Ditto.
JOHN MILLWARD	Ditto.
WILLIAM M'KOY	Ditto.
HENRY HILLBRANT	Ditto.
MICHAEL BYRNE	Ditto.
WILLIAM MUSPRAT	Ditto.
ALEXANDER SMITH	Ditto.
JOHN WILLIAMS	Ditto.
THOMAS ELLISON	Ditto.
ISAAC MARTIN	Ditto.
RICHARD SKINNER	Ditto.
MATTHEW THOMPSON	Ditto.
WILLIAM BROWN	Gardiner.
JOSEPH COLEMAN	Armourer.
CHARLES NORMAN	Carpenter's Mate.
THOMAS M'INTOSH	Carpenter's Crew.

In all 25 hands, and the most able men of the ship's company.

Having little or no wind, we rowed pretty fast towards Tofoa, which bore N E about 10 leagues from us. While the ship was in sight she steered to the W N W, but I considered this only as a feint; for when we were sent away—" Huzza for Otaheite," was frequently heard among the mutineers.

Christian, the captain of the gang, is of a respectable family

mily in the north of England. This was the third voyage he had made with me; and, as I found it neceffary to keep my fhip's company at three watches, I gave him an order to take charge of the third, his abilities being thoroughly equal to the tafk; and by this means my mafter and gunner were not at watch and watch.

Haywood is alfo of a refpectable family in the north of England, and a young man of abilities, as well as Chriftian. Thefe two were objects of my particular regard and attention, and I took great pains to inftruct them, for they really promifed, as profeffional men, to be a credit to their country.

Young was well recommended, and appeared to me an able ftout feaman; therefore I was glad to take him: he, however, fell fhort of what his appearance promifed.

Stewart was a young man of creditable parents, in the Orkneys; at which place, on the return of the Refolution from the South Seas, in 1780, we received fo many civilities, that, on that account only, I fhould gladly have taken him with me: but, independent of this recommendation, he was a feaman, and had always borne a good character.

Notwithftanding the roughnefs with which I was treated, the remembrance of paft kindneffes produced fome figns of remorfe in Chriftian. When they were forcing me out of the fhip, I afked him, if this treatment was a proper return for the many inftances he had received of my friendfhip? he appeared difturbed at my queftion, and anfwered, with much emotion, " That,—captain Bligh,— " that is the thing;——I am in hell—I am in hell."

As foon as I had time to reflect, I felt an inward fatisfaction, which prevented any depreffion of my fpirits: confcious of my integrity, and anxious folicitude for the good

of

of the fervice in which I was engaged, I found my mind wonderfully fupported, and I began to conceive hopes, notwithftanding fo heavy a calamity, that I fhould one day be able to account to my King and country for the misfortune.——A few hours before, my fituation had been peculiarly flattering. I had a fhip in the moft perfect order, and well ftored with every neceffary both for fervice and health: by early attention to thofe particulars I had, as much as lay in my power, provided againft any accident, in cafe I could not get through Endeavour Straits, as well as againft what might befal me in them; add to this, the plants had been fuccefsfully preferved in the moft flourifhing ftate: fo that, upon the whole, the voyage was two thirds completed, and the remaining part in a very promifing way; every perfon on board being in perfect health, to eftablifh which was ever amongft the principal objects of my attention.

It will very naturally be afked, what could be the reafon for fuch a revolt? in anfwer to which, I can only conjecture that the mutineers had affured themfelves of a more happy life among the Otaheiteans, than they could poffibly have in England; which, joined to fome female connections, have moft probably been the principal caufe of the whole tranfaction.

The women at Otaheite are handfome, mild and chearful in their manners and converfation, poffeffed of great fenfibility, and have fufficient delicacy to make them admired and beloved. The chiefs were fo much attached to our people, that they rather encouraged their ftay among them than otherwife, and even made them promifes of large poffeffions. Under thefe, and many other attendant circumftances, equally defirable, it is now perhaps not fo much to be wondered at, though fcarcely poffible to have

C been

been forefeen, that a fet of failors, moft of them void of connections, fhould be led away; efpecially when, in addition to fuch powerful inducements, they imagined it in their power to fix themfelves in the midft of plenty, on the fineft ifland in the world, where they need not labour, and where the allurements of diffipation are beyond any thing that can be conceived. The utmoft, however, that any commander could have fuppofed to have happened is, that fome of the people would have been tempted to defert. But if it fhould be afferted, that a commander is to guard againft an act of mutiny and piracy in his own fhip, more than by the common rules of fervice, it is as much as to fay that he muft fleep locked up, and when awake, be girded with piftols.

Defertions have happened, more or lefs, from many of the fhips that have been at the Society Iflands; but it ever has been in the commanders power to make the chiefs return their people: the knowledge, therefore, that it was unfafe to defert, perhaps, firft led mine to confider with what eafe fo fmall a fhip might be furprized, and that fo favourable an opportunity would never offer to them again.

The fecrecy of this mutiny is beyond all conception. Thirteen of the party, who were with me, had always lived forward among the people; yet neither they, nor the mefsmates of Chriftian, Stewart, Haywood, and Young, had ever obferved any circumftance to give them fufpicion of what was going on. With fuch clofe-planned acts of villainy, and my mind free from any fufpicion, it is not wonderful that I have been got the better of. Perhaps, if I had had marines, a centinel at my cabin-door might have prevented it; for I flept with the door always open, that the officer of the watch might have accefs to me on all occafions. The poffibility

bility of fuch a confpiracy was ever the fartheft from my thoughts. Had their mutiny been occafioned by any grievances, either real or imaginary, I muft have difcovered fymptoms of their difcontent, which would have put me on my guard : but the cafe was far otherwife. Chriftian, in particular, I was on the moft friendly terms with ; that very day he was engaged to have dined with me; and the preceding night he excufed himfelf from fupping with me, on pretence of being unwell ; for which I felt concerned, having no fufpicions of his integrity and honour.

It now remained with me to confider what was beft to be done. My firft determination was to feek a fupply of bread-fruit and water at Tofoa, and afterwards to fail for Tongataboo, and there rifk a folicitation to Poulaho, the king, to equip my boat, and grant a fupply of water and provifions, fo as to enable us to reach the Eaft Indies.

The quantity of provifions I found in the boat was 150 lb. of bread, 16 pieces of pork, each piece weighing 2 lb. 6 quarts of rum, 6 bottles of wine, with 28 gallons of water, and four empty barrecoes.

Wednefday, April 29th *. Happily the afternoon kept calm, until about 4 o'clock, when we were fo far to windward, that, with a moderate eafterly breeze which fprung up, we were able to fail. It was neverthelefs dark when we got to Tofoa, where I expected to land ; but the fhore proved to be fo fteep and rocky, that I was obliged to give up all thoughts of it, and keep the boat under the lee of the ifland with two oars ; for there was no anchorage. Having fixed on this mode of proceeding for the night, I ferved

* It is to be obferved, that the account of time is kept in the nautical way, each day ending at noon Thus the beginning of the 29th of April is, according to the common way of reckoning, the afternoon of the 28th.

to

to every perfon half a pint of grog, and each took to his reft as well as our unhappy fituation would allow.

In the morning, at dawn of day, we fet off along fhore in fearch of landing, and about ten o'clock we dif-covered a ftony cove at the N W part of the ifland, where I dropt the grapnel within 20 yards of the rocks. A great deal of furf ran on the fhore ; but, as I was unwilling to diminifh our ftock of provifions, I landed Mr. Samuel, and fome others, who climbed the cliffs, and got into the country to fearch for fupplies. The reft of us remained at the cove, not difcovering any way to get into the country, but that by which Mr. Samuel had proceeded. It was great confolation to me to find, that the fpirits of my people did not fink, notwithftanding our miferable and almoft hopelefs fituation. Towards noon Mr. Samuel returned, with a few quarts of water, which he had found in holes; but he had met with no fpring, or any profpect of a fufficient fupply in that particular, and had only feen figns of inhabitants. As it was impoffible to know how much we might be in want, I only iffued a morfel of bread, and a glafs of wine, to each perfon for dinner.

I obferved the latitude of this cove to be 19° 41′ S.

This is the N W part of Tofoa, the north-wefternmoft of the Friendly Iflands.

Thurfday, April 30th. Fair weather, but the wind blew fo violently from the E S E that I could not venture to fea. Our detention therefore made it abfolutely neceffary to fee what we could do more for our fupport; for I determined, if poffible, to keep my firft ftock entire : I therefore weighed, and rowed along fhore, to fee if any thing could be got; and at laft difcovered fome cocoa-nut trees, but they were on the top of high precipices, and the furf made it dangerous

ous landing; both one and the other we, however, got the better of. Some, with much difficulty, climbed the cliffs, and got about 20 cocoa-nuts, and others flung them to ropes, by which we hauled them through the furf into the boat. This was all that could be done here; and, as I found no place fo eligible as the one we had left to fpend the night at, I returned to the cove, and, having ferved a cocoa-nut to each perfon, we went to reft again in the boat.

At dawn of day I attempted to get to fea; but the wind and weather proved fo bad, that I was glad to return to my former ftation; where, after iffuing a morfel of bread and a fpoonful of rum to each perfon, we landed, and I went off with Mr. Nelfon, Mr. Samuel, and fome others, into the country, having hauled ourfelves up the precipice by long vines, which were fixed there by the natives for that purpofe; this being the only way into the country.

We found a few deferted huts, and a fmall plantain walk, but little taken care of; from which we could only collect three fmall bunches of plantains. After paffing this place, we came to a deep gully that led towards a mountain, near a volcano; and, as I conceived that in the rainy fea-fon very great torrents of water muft pafs through it, we hoped to find fufficient for our ufe remaining in fome holes of the rocks; but, after all our fearch, the whole that we found was only nine gallons, in the courfe of the day. We advanced within two miles of the foot of the higheft mountain in the ifland, on which is the volcano that is almoft conftantly burning. The country near it is all covered with lava, and has a moft dreary appearance. As we had not been fortunate in our difcoveries, and faw but little to alleviate our diftreffes, we filled our cocoa-nut fhells with the water we found, and returned exceedingly fatigued

gued and faint. When I came to the precipice whence we were to defcend into the cove, I was feized with fuch a dizzinefs in my head, that I thought it fcarce poffible to effect it: however, by the affiftance of Mr. Nelfon and others, they at laft got me down, in a weak condition. Every perfon being returned by noon, I gave about an ounce of pork and two plantains to each, with half a glafs of wine. I again obferved the latitude of this place 19° 41' fouth. The people who remained by the boat I had directed to look for fifh, or what they could pick up about the rocks; but nothing eatable could be found: fo that, upon the whole, we confidered ourfelves on as miferable a fpot of land as could well be imagined.

I could not fay pofitively, from the former knowledge I had of this ifland, whether it was inhabited or not; but I knew it was confidered inferior to the other iflands, and I was not certain but that the Indians only reforted to it at particular times. I was very anxious to afcertain this point; for, in cafe there had only been a few people here, and thofe could have furnifhed us with but very moderate fupplies, the remaining in this fpot to have made preparations for our voyage, would have been preferable to the rifk of going amongft multitudes, where perhaps we might lofe every thing. A party, therefore, fufficiently ftrong, I determined fhould go another route, as foon as the fun became lower; and they cheerfully undertook it.

Friday, May the 1ft: ftormy weather, wind E S E and S E. About two o'clock in the afternoon the party fet out; but, after fuffering much fatigue, they returned in the evening, without any kind of fuccefs.

At the head of the cove, about 150 yards from the water-

water-fide, was a cave; acrofs the ftony beach was about 100 yards, and the only way from the country into the cove was that which I have already defcribed. The fituation fe-cured us from the danger of being furprifed, and I deter-mined to remain on fhore for the night, with a part of my people, that the others might have more room to reft in the boat, with the mafter; whom I directed to lie at a grapnel, and be watchful, in cafe we fhould be attacked. I ordered one plantain for each perfon to be boiled; and, having fupped on this fcanty allowance, with a quarter of a pint of grog, and fixed the watches for the night, thofe whofe turn it was, laid down to fleep in the cave; before which we kept up a good fire, yet notwithftanding we were much troubled with flies and mufquitoes.

At dawn of day the party fet out again in a different route, to fee what they could find; in the courfe of which they fuffered greatly for want of water: they, however, met with two men, a woman, and a child; the men came with them to the cove, and brought two cocoa-nut fhells of water. I immediately made friends with thefe people, and fent them away for bread-fruit, plantains, and water. Soon after other natives came to us; and by noon I had 30 of them about me, trading with the articles we were in want of: but I could only afford one ounce of pork, and a quarter of a bread-fruit, to each man for dinner, with half a pint of water; for I was fixed in not ufing any of the bread or water in the boat.

No particular chief was yet among the natives: they were, notwithftanding, tractable, and behaved honeftly, giving the provifions they brought for a few buttons and beads. The party who had been out, informed me of having difcovered feveral neat plantations; fo that it became

came no longer a doubt of there being settled inhabitants on the island; and for that reason I determined to get what I could, and sail the first moment the wind and weather would allow me to put to sea.

Saturday, May the 2d: stormy weather, wind E S E It had hitherto been a weighty consideration with me, how I was to account to the natives for the loss of my ship: I knew they had too much sense to be amused with a story that the ship was to join me, when she was not in sight from the hills. I was at first doubtful whether I should tell the real fact, or say that the ship had overset and sunk, and that only we were saved: the latter appeared to me to be the most proper and advantageous to us, and I accordingly instructed my people, that we might all agree in one story. As I expected, enquiries were made after the ship, and they seemed readily satisfied with our account; but there did not appear the least symptom of joy or sorrow in their faces, although I fancied I discovered some marks of surprise. Some of the natives were coming and going the whole afternoon, and we got enough of bread-fruit, plantains, and cocoa-nuts for another day; but water they only brought us about five pints. A canoe also came in with four men, and brought a few cocoa-nuts and bread-fruit, which I bought as I had done the rest. Nails were much enquired after, but I would not suffer one to be shewn, as I wanted them for the use of the boat.

Towards evening I had the satisfaction to find our stock of provisions somewhat increased: but the natives did not appear to have much to spare. What they brought was in such small quantities, that I had no reason to hope we should be able to procure from them sufficient to stock us for our voyage. At sunset all the natives left us in

quiet

quiet poffeffion of the cove. I thought this a good fign, and made no doubt that they would come again the next day with a larger proportion of food and water, with which I hoped to fail without farther delay : for if, in attempting to get to Tongataboo, we fhould be blown away from the iflands altogether, there would be a larger quantity of provifions to fupport us againft fuch a misfortune.

At night I ferved a quarter of a bread-fruit and a cocoa-nut to each perfon for fupper ; and, a good fire being made, all but the watch went to fleep.

At day-break I was happy to find every one's fpirits a little revived, and that they no longer regarded me with thofe anxious looks, which had conftantly been directed towards me fince we loft fight of the fhip : every countenance appeared to have a degree of cheerfulnefs, and they all feemed determined to do their beft.

As I doubted of water being brought by the natives, I fent a party among the gullies in the mountains, with empty fhells, to fee what they could get. In their abfence the natives came about us, as I expected, but more numerous ; alfo two canoes came in from round the north fide of the ifland. In one of them was an elderly chief, called Maccaackavow. Soon after fome of our foraging party returned, and with them came a good-looking chief, called Eegijeefow, or perhaps more properly Eefow, Egij or Eghee, fignifying a chief. To both thefe men I made a prefent of an old fhirt and a knife, and I foon found they either had feen me, or had heard of my being at Annamooka. They knew I had been with captain Cook, who they enquired after, and alfo captain Clerk. They were very inquifitive to know in what manner I had

D

loft

loft my ſhip. During this converſation a young man appeared, whom I remembered to have ſeen at Annamooka,
called Nageete: he expreſſed much pleaſure at ſeeing me.
I now enquired after Poulaho and Feenow, who, they ſaid,
were at Tongataboo; and Eefow agreed to accompany
me thither, if I would wait till the weather moderated. The
readineſs and affability of this man gave me much ſatiſ-
faction.

This, however, was but of ſhort duration, for the natives began to increaſe in number, and I obſerved ſome
ſymptoms of a deſign againſt us; ſoon after they attempted
to haul the boat on ſhore, when I threatened Eefow with a
cutlaſs, to induce him to make them deſiſt; which they did,
and every thing became quiet again. My people, who had
been in the mountains, now returned with about three gallons of water. I kept buying up the little bread-fruit that
was brought to us, and likewiſe ſome ſpears to arm my men
with, having only four cutlaſſes, two of which were in the
boat. As we had no means of improving our ſituation, I
told our people I would wait until ſun-ſet, by which
time, perhaps, ſomething might happen in our favour:
that if we attempted to go at preſent, we muſt fight our
way through, which we could do more advantageouſly at
night; and that in the mean time we would endeavour to
get off to the boat what we had bought. The beach was
now lined with the natives, and we heard nothing but the
knocking of ſtones together, which they had in each hand.
I knew very well this was the ſign of an attack. It being now noon, I ſerved a cocoa-nut and a bread-fruit to
each perſon for dinner, and gave ſome to the chiefs, with
whom I continued to appear intimate and friendly. They

frequently

frequently importuned me to fit down, but I as conftantly refufed; for it occured both to Mr. Nelfon and myfelf, that they intended to feize hold of me, if I gave them fuch an opportunity. Keeping, therefore, conftantly on our guard, we were fuffered to eat our uncomfortable meal in fome quietnefs.

1789. MAY 2.

Sunday, 3d May, frefh gales at S E and E S E, varying to the N E in the latter part, with a ftorm of wind.

Sunday 3.

After dinner we began by little and little to get our things into the boat, which was a troublefome bufinefs, on account of the furf. I carefully watched the motions of the natives, who ftill increafed in number, and found that, inftead of their intention being to leave us, fires were made, and places fixed on for their ftay during the night. Confultations were alfo held among them, and every thing affured me we fhould be attacked. I fent orders to the mafter, that when he faw us coming down, he fhould keep the boat clofe to the fhore, that we might the more readily embark.

I had my journal on fhore with me, writing the occurrences in the cave, and in fending it down to the boat it was nearly fnatched away, but for the timely affiftance of the gunner.

The fun was near fetting when I gave the word, on which every perfon, who was on fhore with me, boldly took up his proportion of things, and carried them to the boat. The chiefs afked me if I would not ftay with them all night, I faid, " No, I never fleep out of my boat; but in " the morning we will again trade with you, and I fhall " remain until the weather is moderate, that we may go, " as we have agreed, to fee Poulaho, at Tongataboo." Maccaackavow then got up, and faid, " You will not fleep

" on

" on fhore? then Mattie," (which directly fignifies we will kill you) and he left me. The onfet was now preparing; every one, as I have defcribed before, kept knocking ftones together, and Eefow quitted me. We had now all but two or three things in the boat, when I took Nageete by the hand, and we walked down the beach, every one in à filent kind of horror.

When I came to the boat, and was feeing the people embark, Nageete wanted me to ftay to fpeak to Eefow; but I found he was encouraging them to the attack, and I determined, had it then begun, to have killed him for his treacherous behaviour. I ordered the carpenter not to quit me until the other people were in the boat. Nageete, finding I would not ftay, loofed himfelf from my hold and went off, and we all got into the boat except one man, who, while I was getting on board, quitted it, and ran up the beach to caft the ftern faft off, notwithftanding the mafter and others called to him to return, while they were hauling me out of the water.

I was no fooner in the boat than the attack began by about 200 men; the unfortunate poor man who had run up the beach was knocked down, and the ftones flew like a fhower of fhot. Many Indians got hold of the ftern rope, and were near hauling us on fhore, and would certainly have done it if I had not had a knife in my pocket, with which I cut the rope. We then hauled off to the grapnel, every one being more or lefs hurt. At this time I faw five of the natives about the poor man they had killed, and two of them were beating him about the head with ftones in their hands.

We had no time to reflect, before, to my furprife, they
filled

filled their canoes with ftones, and twelve men came off after us to renew the attack, which they did fo effectually as nearly to difable all of us. Our grapnel was foul, but Providence here affifted us; the fluke broke, and we got to our oars, and pulled to fea. They, however, could paddle round us, fo that we were obliged to fuftain the attack without being able to return it, except with fuch ftones as lodged in the boat, and in this I found we were very inferior to them. We could not clofe, becaufe our boat was lumbered and heavy, and that they knew very well: I therefore adopted the expedient of throwing overboard fome cloaths, which they loft time in picking up; and, as it was now almoft dark, they gave over the attack, and returned towards the fhore, leaving us to reflect on our unhappy fituation.

The poor man I loft was John Norton: this was his fecond voyage with me as a quarter-mafter, and his worthy character made me lament his lofs very much. He has left an aged parent, I am told, whom he fupported.

I once before fuftained an attack of a fimilar nature, with a fmaller number of Europeans, againft a multitude of Indians; it was after the death of captain Cook, on the Morai at Owhyhee, where I was left by lieutenant King: yet, notwithftanding, I did not conceive that the power of a man's arm could throw ftones, from two to eight pounds weight, with fuch force and exactnefs as thefe people did. Here unhappily I was without arms, and the Indians knew it; but it was a fortunate circumftance that they did not begin to attack us in the cave: in that cafe our deftruction muft have been inevitable, and we fhould have had nothing left for it but to die as bravely as we could, fighting clofe together; in which I found every

one

one cheerfully difpofed to join me. This appearance of refolution deterred them, fuppofing they could effect their purpofe without rifk after we were in the boat.

Taking this as a fample of the difpofitions of the Indians, there was little reafon to expect much benefit if I perfevered in my intention of vifiting Poulaho; for I confidered their good behaviour hitherto to proceed from a dread of our fire-arms, which, now knowing us deftitute of, would ceafe; and, even fuppofing our lives not in danger, the boat and every thing we had would moft probably be taken from us, and thereby all hopes precluded of ever being able to return to our native country.

We were now failing along the weft fide of the ifland Tofoa, and my mind was employed in confidering what was beft to be done, when I was folicited by all hands to take them towards home: and, when I told them no hopes of relief for us remained, but what I might find at New Holland, until I came to Timor, a diftance of full 1200 leagues, where was a Dutch fettlement, but in what part of the ifland I knew not, they all agreed to live on one ounce of bread, and a quarter of a pint of water, per day. Therefore, after examining our ftock of provifions, and recommending this as a facred promife for ever to their memory, we bore away acrofs a fea, where the navigation is but little known, in a fmall boat, twenty-three feet long from ftem to ftern, deep laden with eighteen men; without a chart, and nothing but my own recollection and general knowledge of the fituation of places, affifted by a book of latitudes and longitudes, to guide us. I was happy, however, to fee every one better fatisfied with our fituation in this particular than myfelf.

Our ftock of provifions confifted of about one hundred and fifty pounds of bread, twenty-eight gallons of water, twenty
pounds

pounds of pork, three bottles of wine, and five quarts of rum. The difference between this and the quantity we had on leaving the ship, was principally owing to lofs in the buftle and confufion of the attack. A few cocoa-nuts were in the boat, and fome bread-fruit, but the latter was trampled to pieces.

It was about eight o'clock at night when I bore away under a reefed lug fore-fail : and, having divided the people into watches, and got the boat in a little order, we returned God thanks for our miraculous prefervation, and, fully confident of his gracious fupport, I found my mind more at eafe than for fome time paft.

At day-break the gale increafed; the fun rofe very fiery and red, a fure indication of a fevere gale of wind. At eight it blew a violent ftorm, and the fea ran very high, fo that between the feas the fail was becalmed, and when on the top of the fea it was too much to have fet: but I was obliged to carry to it, for we were now in very imminent danger and diftrefs, the fea curling over the ftern of the boat, which obliged us to bale with all our might. A fituation more diftreffing has, perhaps, feldom been experienced.

Our bread was in bags, and in danger of being fpoiled by the wet: to be ftarved to death was inevitable, if this could not be prevented : I therefore began to examine what cloaths there were in the boat, and what other things could be fpared; and, having determined that only two fuits fhould be kept for each perfon, the reft was thrown overboard, with fome rope and fpare fails, which lightened the boat confiderably, and we had more room to bale the water out. Fortunately the carpenter had a good cheft in the boat, into which I put the bread the firft favourable moment.

moment. His tool cheft alſo was cleared, and the tools ſtowed in the bottom of the boat, ſo that this became a ſecond convenience.

I now ſerved a tea-ſpoonful of rum to each perſon, (for we were very wet and cold) with a quarter of a bread-fruit, which was ſcarce eatable, for dinner; but our engagement was now ſtrictly to be carried into execution, and I was fully determined to make what proviſions I had laſt eight weeks, let the daily proportion be ever ſo ſmall.

At noon I conſidered my courſe and diſtance from Tofoa to be W N W ¼ W. 86 miles, my latitude 19° 27′ S. I directed my courſe to the W N W, that I might get a ſight of the iſlands called Feejee, if they laid in the direction the natives had pointed out to me.

Monday, 4th May. This day the weather was very ſevere, it blew a ſtorm from N E to E S E. The ſea ran higher than yeſterday, and the fatigue of baling, to keep the boat from filling, was exceedingly great. We could do nothing more than keep before the ſea; in the courſe of which the boat performed ſo wonderfully well, that I no longer dreaded any danger in that reſpect. But among the hardſhips we were to undergo, that of being conſtantly wet was not the leaſt: the nights were very cold, and at day-light our limbs were ſo benumbed, that we could ſcarce find the uſe of them. At this time I ſerved a tea-ſpoonful of rum to each perſon, which we all found great benefit from.

As I have mentioned before, I determined to keep to the W N W, until I got more to the northward, for I not only expected to have better weather, but to ſee the Feejee Iſlands, as I have often underſtood, from the natives of Annamooka,

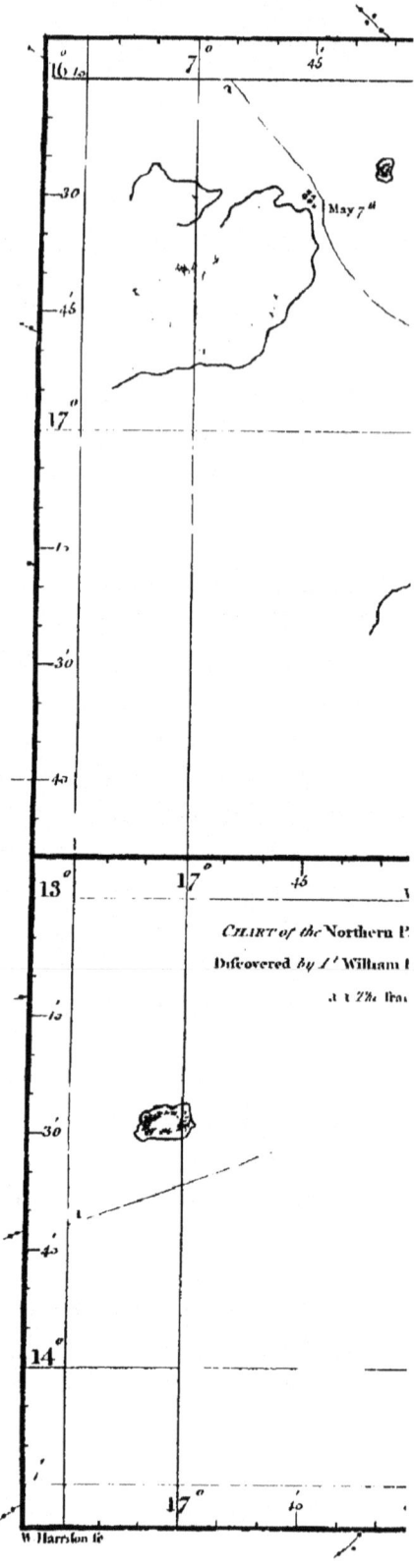

CHART of the Northern P.
Discovered by L.' William I
.. t 7th Ira.

W Harriston fe

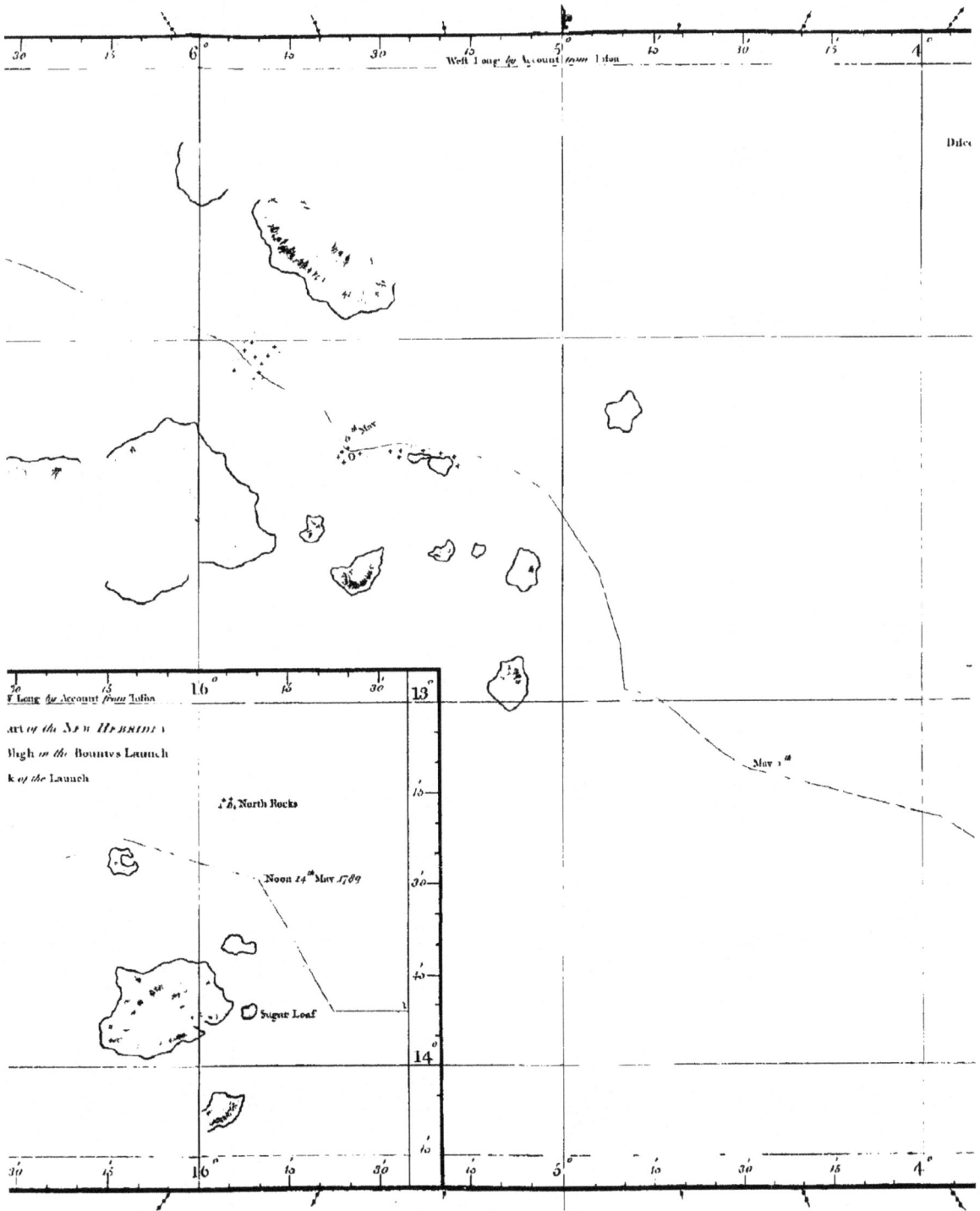

West Long.r by Account from Tofua

30   15   6°   10   30   5°   15   4°

Dire

E Long.r by Account from Tofua

30   15   16°   15   30   13°

art of the New Hebrides

high in the Bountys Launch

k of the Launch

North Rocks

Noon 24th May 1789

Sugar Loaf

15

30

40

14°

15

30   15   16°   10   30   5°   10   30   15   4°

May 1st

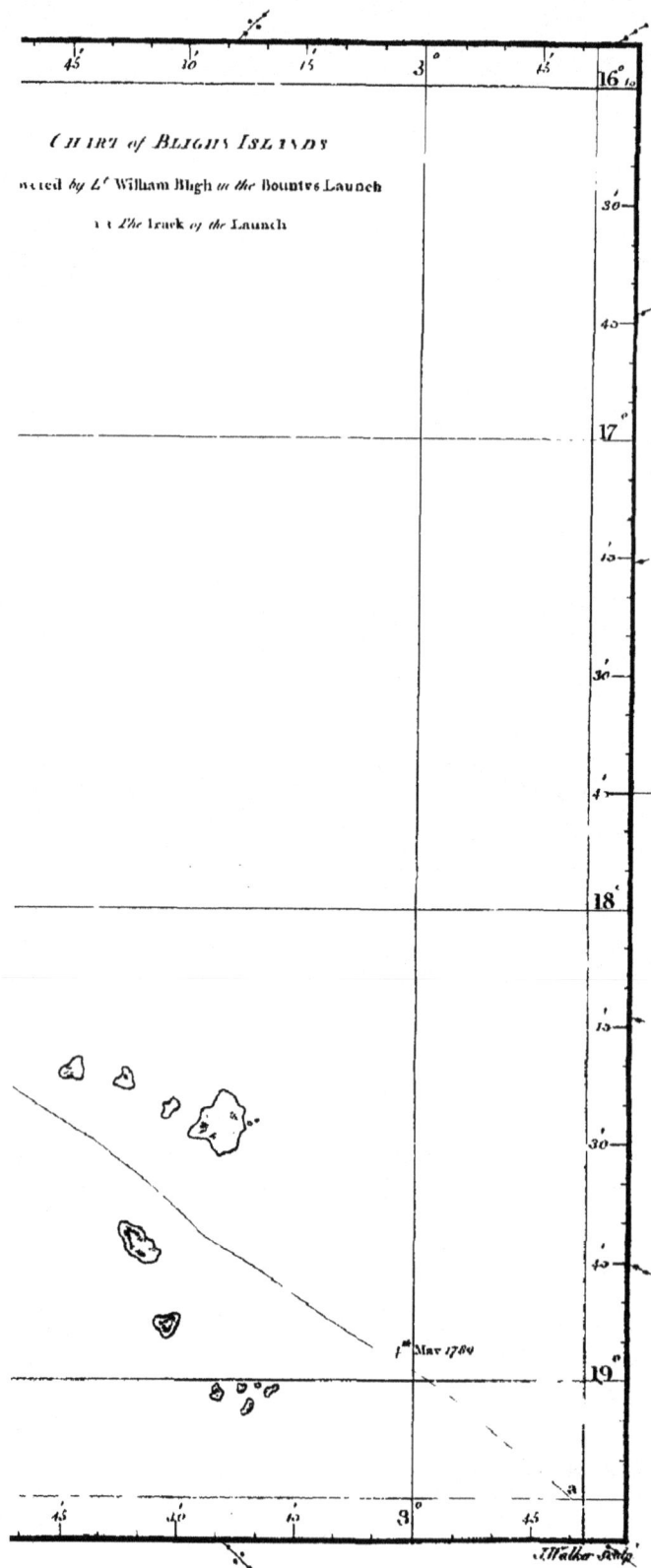

CHART of BLIGHS ISLANDS

...ed by L.t William Bligh in the Bountys Launch

... the track of the Launch

1st May 1789

J. Walker Sculp.

namooka, that they lie in that direction; Captain Cook like-wife confiders them to be N W by W from Tongataboo. Juſt before noon we difcovered a fmall flat iſland of a moderate height, bearing W S W, 4 or 5 leagues. I obferved in la-titude 18° 58′ S; our longitude, by account, 3° 4′ W from the iſland Tofoa, having made a N 72° W courfe, diſtance 95 miles, fince yefterday noon. I divided five fmall cocoa-nuts for our dinner, and every one was fatisfied.

Tuefday, 5th May. Towards the evening the gale confi-derably abated. Wind S E.

A little after noon, other iſlands appeared, and at a quar-ter paſt three o'clock we could count eight, bearing from S round by the weſt to N W by N; thofe to the fouth, which were the neareſt, being four leagues diſtant from us.

I kept my courfe to the N W by W, between the iſlands, and at fix o'clock difcovered three other fmall iſlands to the N W, the weſternmoſt of them bore N W ¼ W 7 leagues. I ſteered to the fouthward of thefe iſlands, a W N W courfe for the night, under a reefed fail.

Served a few broken pieces of bread-fruit for fupper, and performed prayers.

The night turned out fair, and, having had tolerable reſt, every one feemed confiderably better in the morning, and contentedly breakfaſted on a few pieces of yams that were found in the boat. After breakfaſt we prepared a cheſt for our bread, and got it fecured: but unfortunately a great deal was damaged and rotten; this neverthelefs we were glad to keep for ufe.

I had hitherto been fcarcely able to keep any account of our run; but we now equipped ourfelves a little bet-ter, by getting a log-line marked, and, having practifed at

E   counting

counting feconds, feveral could do it with fome degree of exactnefs.

The iflands I have paffed lie between the latitude of 19° 5′ S and 18° 19′ S, and, according to my reckoning, from 3° 17′ to 3° 46′ W longitude from the ifland Tofoa: the largeft may be about fix leagues in circuit; but it is impoffible for me to be very exact. To fhow where they are to be found again is the moft my fituation enabled me to do. The fketch I have made, will give a comparative view of their extent. I believe all the larger iflands are inhabited, as they appeared very fertile.

At noon I obferved, in latitude 18° 10′ S, and confidered my courfe and diftance from yefterday noon, N W by W ¼ W, 94 miles; longitude, by account, from Tofoa 4° 29′ W.

For dinner, I ferved fome of the damaged bread, and a quarter of a pint of water.

Wednefday, 6th May. Frefh breezes E N E, and fair weather, but very hazy.

About fix o'clock this afternoon I difcovered two iflands, one bearing W by S 6 leagues, and the other N W by N 8 leagues; I kept to windward of the northernmoft, and paffing it by 10 o'clock, I refumed my courfe to the N W and W N W. At day-light in the morning I difcovered a number of other iflands from S S E to the W, and round to N E by E; between thofe in the N W I determined to pafs. At noon a fmall fandy ifland or key, 2 miles diftant from me, bore from E to S ¼ W. I had paffed ten iflands, the largeft of which may be 6 or 8 leagues in circuit. Much larger lands appeared in the S W and N by W, between which I directed my courfe. Latitude obferved 17° 17′ S; courfe fince yefterday noon N 50° W; diftance 84 miles; longitude made, by account, 5° 37′ W.

Our

Our fupper, breakfaft, and dinner, confifted of a quarter of a pint of cocoa-nut milk, and the meat, which did not exceed two ounces to each perfon: it was received very contentedly, but we fuffered great drought. I dared not to land, as we had no arms, and were lefs capable to defend ourfelves than we were at Tofoa.

To keep an account of the boat's run was rendered difficult, from being conftantly wet with the fea breaking over us; but, as we advanced towards the land, the fea became fmoother, and I was enabled to form a fketch of the iflands, which will ferve to give a general knowledge of their extent. Thofe I have been near are fruitful and hilly, fome very mountainous, and all of a good height.

To our great joy we hooked a fifh, but we were miferably difappointed by its being loft in getting into the boat.

Thurfday, 7th May. Variable weather and cloudy, wind north-eafterly, and calms. I continued my courfe to the N W, between the iflands, which, by the evening, appeared of confiderable extent, woody, and mountainous. At funfet the foutherumoft bore from S to S W by W, and the northernmoft from N by W ¼ W to N E ¾ E. At fix o'clock I was nearly mid-way between them, and about 6 leagues diftant from each fhore, when I fell in with a coral bank, where I had only four feet water, without the leaft break on it, or ruffle of the fea to give us warning. I could only fee that it extended about a mile on each fide of us; but, as it is probable that it extends much farther, I have laid it down fo in my fketch.

I now directed my courfe W by N for the night, and ferved to each perfon an ounce of the damaged bread, and a quarter of a pint of water, for fupper.

It may readily be fuppofed, that our lodgings were very

miferable

miferable and confined, and I had only in my power to remedy the latter defect by putting ourfelves at watch and
watch; fo that one half always fat up while the other lay
down on the boat's bottom, or upon a cheft, with nothing
to cover us but the heavens. Our limbs were dreadfully
cramped, for we could not ftretch them out, and the nights
were fo cold, and we fo conftantly wet, that after a few hours
fleep we could fcarce move.

At dawn of day we again difcovered land from W S W
to W N W, and another ifland N N W, the latter a high
round lump of but little extent; and I could fee the fouth-
ern land that I had paffed in the night. Being very wet
and cold, I ferved a fpoonful of rum and a morfel of
bread for breakfaft.

As I advanced towards the land in the weft, it appeared
in a variety of forms; fome extraordinary high rocks, and
the country agreeably interfperfed with high and low land,
covered in fome places with wood. Off the N E part lay
two fmall rocky iflands, between which and the ifland to the
N E, 4 leagues apart, I directed my courfe; but a lee current
very unexpectedly fet us very near to the fhore, and I could
only get clear of it by rowing, paffing clofe to the reef that
furrounded the rocky ifles. We now obferved two large
failing canoes coming fwiftly after us along fhore, and,
being apprehenfive of their intentions, we rowed with fome
anxiety, being fenfible of our weak and defencelefs ftate.
It was now noon, calm and cloudy weather, my latitude is
therefore doubtful to 3 or 4 miles; my courfe fince yefterday
noon N 56 W, diftance 79 miles; latitude by account, 16° 29' S,
and longitude by account, from Tofoa, 6° 46' W. Being
conftantly wet, it was with the utmoft difficulty I could
open a book to write, and I am fenfible that what I have
done

done can only ferve to point out where thefe lands are to be found again, and give an idea of their extent.

Friday, 8th May. All the afternoon the weather was very rainy, attended with thunder and lightning. Wind N N E.

Only one of the canoes gained upon us, and by three o'clock in the afternoon was not more than two miles off, when fhe gave over chafe.

If I may judge from the fail of the veffels, they are the fame as at the Friendly Iflands, and the nearnefs of their fituation leaves little room to doubt of their being the fame kind of people. Whether thefe canoes had any hoftile intention againft us is a matter of doubt; perhaps we might have benefited by an intercourfe with them, but in our defencelefs fituation it would have been rifking too much to make the experiment.

I imagine thefe to be the iflands called Feejee, as their extent, direction, and diftance from the Friendly Iflands, anfwers to the defcription given of them by thofe Iflanders. Heavy rain came on at four o'clock, when every perfon did their utmoft to catch fome water, and we increafed our ftock to 34 gallons, befides quenching our thirft for the firft time fince we had been at fea; but an attendant confequence made us pafs the night very miferably, for, being extremely wet, and no dry things to fhift or cover us, we experienced cold and fhiverings fcarce to be conceived. Moft fortunately for us, the forenoon turned out fair, and we ftripped and dried our cloaths. The allowance I iffued to-day, was an ounce and a half of pork, a tea-fpoonful of rum, half a pint of cocoa-nut milk, and an ounce of bread. The rum, though fo fmall in quantity, was of the greateft fervice. A fifhing-line was generally towing, and we faw great numbers of fifh, but could never catch one.

At noon, I obferved, in latitude 16° 4′ S, and found I had
made.

made a courfe, from yefterday noon, N 62° W, diftance 62 miles; longitude, by account, from Tofoa, 7° 42' W.

The land I paffed yefterday, and the day before, is a group of iflands, 14 or 16 in number, lying between the latitude of 16° 26' S and 17° 57' S, and in longitude, by my account, 4° 47' to 7° 17' W from Tofoa; three of thefe iflands are very large, having from 30 to 40 leagues of fea-coaft.

Saturday 9.
Saturday, 9th May. Fine weather, and light winds from the N E to E by S.

This afternoon we cleaned out the boat, and it employed us till fun-fet to get every thing dry and in order. Hitherto I had iffued the allowance by guefs, but I now got a pair of fcales, made with two cocoa-nut fhells; and, having accidentally fome piftol-balls in the boat, 25 * of which weighed one pound, or 16 ounces, I adopted one, as the proportion of weight that each perfon fhould receive of bread at the times I ferved it. I alfo amufed all hands, with defcribing the fituation of New Guinea and New Holland, and gave them every information in my power, that in cafe any accident happened to me, thofe who furvived might have fome idea of what they were about, and be able to find their way to Timor, which at prefent they knew nothing of, more than the name, and fome not that.

At night I ferved a quarter of a pint of water, and half an ounce of bread, for fupper. In the morning, a quarter of a pint of cocoa-nut milk, and fome of the decayed bread, for breakfaft; and for dinner, I divided the meat of four cocoa-nuts, with the remainder of the rotten bread, which was only eatable by fuch diftreffed people.

At noon, I obferved the latitude to be 15° 47' S; courfe fince yefterday N 75° W; diftant 64 miles; longitude made, by account, 8° 45' W.

* It weighed 272 grains.

Sunday,

Sunday, May the 10th. The firſt part of this day fine weather; but after ſun-ſet it became ſqually, with hard rain, thunder, and lightning, and a freſh gale; wind E by S, S E, and S S E.

In the afternoon I got fitted a pair of ſhrouds for each maſt and contrived a canvaſs weather cloth round the boat, and raiſed the quarters about nine inches, by nailing on the ſeats of the ſtern ſheets, which proved of great benefit to us.

About nine o'clock in the evening, the clouds began to ga-ther, and we had a prodigious fall of rain, with ſevere thun-der and lightning. By midnight we had caught about twenty gallons of water. Being miſerably wet and cold, I ſerved to each perſon a tea-ſpoonful of rum, to enable them to bear with their diſtreſſed ſituation. The weather continu-ed extremely bad, and the wind increaſed; we ſpent a very miſerable night, without ſleep, but ſuch as could be got in the midſt of rain. The day brought us no relief but its light. The ſea was conſtantly breaking over us, which kept two perſons baling; and we had no choice how to ſteer, for we were obliged to keep before the waves to avoid filling the boat.

The allowance which I now regularly ſerved to each perſon was one 25th of a pound of bread, and a quarter of a pint of water, at ſun-ſet, eight in the morning, and at noon. To-day I gave about half an ounce of pork for dinner, which, though any moderate perſon would have conſidered but a mouthful, was divided into three or four.

The rain abated towards noon, and I obſerved the lati-tude to be 15° 17′ S; courſe N 🏼° W; diſtance 78 miles; longitude made 10° W.

Monday, May the 11th. Strong gales from S S E to S E, and very ſqually weather, with a high breaking ſea, ſo that we were miſerably wet, and ſuffered great cold in the night.

night. In the morning at day-break I ferved to every per-fon a tea-fpoonful of rum, our limbs being fo cramped that we could fcarce feel the ufe of them. Our fituation was now extremely dangerous, the fea frequently running over our ftern, which kept us baling with all our ftrength.

At noon the fun appeared, which gave us as much plea-fure as in a winter's day in England. I iffued the 25th of a pound of bread, and a quarter of a pint of water, as yefterday. Latitude obferved 14° 50′ S; courfe N 71° W; diftance 102 miles; and longitude, by account, 11° 39′ W. from Tofoa.

Tuefday, May the 12th. Strong gales at S E, with much rain and dark difmal weather, moderating towards noon, and wind varying to the N E.

Having again experienced a dreadful night, the day fhow-ed to me a poor miferable fet of beings full of wants, with-out any thing to relieve them. Some complained of a great pain in their bowels, and all of having but very little ufe of their limbs. What fleep we got was fcarce refrefhing, we being covered with fea and rain. Two perfons were obliged to be always baling the water out of the boat. I ferved a fpoonful of rum at day-dawn, and the ufual al-lowance of bread and water, for fupper, breakfaft, and dinner.

At noon it was almoft calm, no fun to be feen, and fome of us fhivering with cold. Courfe fince yefterday W by N; diftance 89 miles; latitude, by account, 14° 33′ S; longitude made 13° 9′ W. The direction of my courfe is to pafs to the northward of the New Hebrides.

Wednefday, May the 13th. Very fqually weather, wind foutherly. As I faw no profpect of getting our cloaths dried, I recommended it to every one to ftrip, and wring them through the falt water, by which means they received

a warmth

a warmth, that, while wet with rain, they could not have, and we were lefs liable to fuffer from colds or rheumatic complaints.

In the afternoon we faw a kind of fruit on the water, which Mr. Nelfon knew to be the Barringtonia of Forfter, and, as I faw the fame again in the morning, and fome men of war birds, I was led to believe we were not far from land.

We continued conftantly fhipping feas, and baling, and were very wet and cold in the night; but I could not afford the allowance of rum at day-break. The twenty-fifth of a pound of bread, and water I ferved as ufual. At noon I had a fight of the fun, latitude 14° 17′ S; courfe W by N 79 miles; longitude made 14° 28′ W.

Thurfday, May the 14th. Frefh breezes and cloudy weather, wind foutherly. Conftantly fhipping water, and very wet, fuffering much cold and fhiverings in the night. Served the ufual allowance of bread and water, three times a day.

At fix in the morning, we faw land, from S W by S eight leagues, to N W by W ¼ W fix leagues, which I foon after found to be four iflands, all of them high and remarkable. At noon difcovered a rocky ifland N W by N four leagues, and another ifland W eight leagues, fo that the whole were fix in number; the four I had firft feen bearing from S ¼ E to S W by S; our diftance three leagues from the neareft ifland. My latitude obferved was 13° 29′ S, and longitude, by account, from Tofoa, 15° 49′ W; courfe fince yefterday noon N 63° W; diftance 89 miles.

Friday, May the 15th. Frefh gales at S E, and gloomy weather with rain, and a very high fea; two people conftantly employed baling.

F   At

At four in the afternoon I paſſed the weſternmoſt iſland. At one in the morning I diſcovered another, bearing W N W, five leagues diſtance, and at eight o'clock I ſaw it for the laſt time, bearing · N E ſeven leagues. A number of gannets, boobies, and men of war birds were ſeen.

Theſe iſlands lie between the latitude of 13° 16′ S and 14° 10′ S: their longitude, according to my reckoning, 15° 51′ to 17° 6′ W from the iſland Tofoa *. The largeſt iſland may be twenty leagues in circuit, the others five or ſix. The eaſternmoſt is the ſmalleſt iſland, and moſt remarkable, having a high ſugar-loaf hill.

The ſight of theſe iſlands ſerved but to increaſe the miſery of our ſituation. We were very little better than ſtarving, with plenty in view; yet to attempt procuring any relief was attended with ſo much danger, that prolonging of life, even in the midſt of miſery, was thought preferable, while there remained hopes of being able to ſurmount our hardſhips. For my own part, I conſider the general run of cloudy and wet weather to be a bleſſing of Providence. Hot weather would have cauſed us to have died with thirſt; and perhaps being ſo conſtantly covered with rain or ſea protected us from that dreadful calamity.

As I had nothing to aſſiſt my memory, I could not determine whether theſe iſlands were a part of the New Hebrides or not: I believed them perfectly a new diſcovery, which I have ſince found to be the caſe; but, though they were not ſeen either by Monſieur Bougainville or Captain Cook, they are ſo nearly in the neighbourhood of the New Hebrides, that they muſt be conſidered as part of the ſame group. They are fertile, and inhabited, as I ſaw ſmoke in ſeveral places.

* By making a proportional allowance for the error afterwards found in the dead reckoning, I eſtimate the longitude of theſe iſlands to be from 167° 17′ E to 168° 34′ E from Greenwich.

Saturday,

Saturday, May the 16th. Frefh gales from the S E, and rainy weather. The night was very dark, not a ftar to be feen to fteer by, and the fea breaking conftantly over us. I found it neceffary to act as much as poffible againft the foutherly winds, to prevent being driven too near New Guinea; for in general we were forced to keep fo much before the fea, that if we had not, at intervals of moderate weather, fteered a more foutherly courfe, we fhould inevitably, from a continuance of the gales, have been thrown in fight of that coaft: in which cafe there would moft probably have been an end to our voyage.

In addition to our miferable allowance of one 25th of a pound of bread, and a quarter of a pint of water, I iffued for dinner about an ounce of falt pork to each perfon. I was often folicited for this pork, but I confidered it better to give it in fmall quantities than to ufe all at once or twice, which would have been done if I had allowed it.

At noon I obferved, in 13° 33′ S; longitude made from Tofoa, 19° 27′ W; courfe N 82° W; diftance 101 miles. The fun gave us hopes of drying our wet cloaths.

Sunday, May the 17th. The funfhine was but of fhort duration. We had ftrong breezes at S E by S, and dark gloomy weather, with ftorms of thunder, lightning, and rain The night was truly horrible, and not a ftar to be feen; fo that our fteerage was uncertain. At dawn of day I found every perfon complaining, and fome of them foliciting extra allowance; but I pofitively refufed it. Our fituation was extremely miferable; always wet, and fuffering extreme cold in the night, without the leaft fhelter from the weather. Being conftantly obliged to bale, to keep the boat from filling, was, perhaps, not to be reckoned an evil, as it gave us exercife.

F 2

The

1789
MAY 17.

The little rum I had was of great service to us; when our nights were particularly diſtreſſing, I generally ſerved a tea-ſpoonful or two to each perſon: and it was always joyful tidings when they heard of my intentions.

At noon a water-ſpout was very near on board of us. I iſſued an ounce of pork, in addition to the allowance of bread and water; but before we began to eat, every perſon ſtript and wrung their cloaths through the ſea-water, which we found warm and refreſhing. Courſe ſince yeſterday noon W S W; diſtance 100 miles; latitude, by account, 14° 11′ S, and longitude made 21° 3′ W.

Monday
18.

Monday, May the 18th. Freſh gales with rain, and a dark diſmal night, wind S E; the ſea conſtantly breaking over us, and nothing but the wind and ſea to direct our ſteerage. I now fully determined to make New Holland, to the ſouthward of Endeavour ſtraits, ſenſible that it was neceſſary to preſerve ſuch a ſituation as would make a ſoutherly wind a fair one; that I might range the reefs until an opening ſhould be found into ſmooth water, and we the ſooner be able to pick up ſome refreſhments.

In the morning the rain abated, when we ſtripped, and wrung our cloaths through the ſea-water, as uſual, which refreſhed us wonderfully. Every perſon complained of violent pain in their bones: I was only ſurpriſed that no one was yet laid up. Served one 25th of a pound of bread, and a quarter of a pint of water, at ſupper, breakfaſt, and dinner, as cuſtomary.

At noon I deduced my ſituation, by account, for we had no glimpſe of the ſun, to be in latitude 14° 52′ S; courſe ſince yeſterday noon W S W 106 miles; longitude made from Tofoa 22° 45′ W. Saw many boobies and noddies, a ſign of being in the neighbourhood of land.

Tueſday,

Tuesday, May the 19th. Fresh gales at E N E, with heavy rain, and dark gloomy weather, and no sight of the sun. We past this day miserably wet and cold, covered with rain and sea, from which we had no relief, but at intervals by pulling off our cloaths and wringing them through the sea water. In the night we had very severe lightning, but otherwise it was so dark that we could not see each other. The morning produced many complaints on the severity of the weather, and I would gladly have issued my allowance of rum, if it had not appeared to me that we were to suffer much more, and that it was necessary to preserve the little I had, to give relief at a time we might be less able to bear such hardships; but, to make up for it, I served out about half an ounce of pork to each person, with the common allowance of bread and water, for dinner. All night and day we were obliged to bale without intermission.

At noon it was very bad weather and constant rain ; latitude, by account, 14° 37′ S ; course since yesterday N 81° W ; distance 100 miles ; longitude made 24° 30′ W.

Wednesday, May the 20th. Fresh breezes E N E with constant rain; at times a deluge. Always baling.

At dawn of day, some of my people seemed half dead : our appearances were horrible ; and I could look no way, but I caught the eye of some one in distress. Extreme hunger was now too evident, but no one suffered from thirst, nor had we much inclination to drink, that desire, perhaps, being satisfied through the skin. The little sleep we got was in the midst of water, and we constantly awoke with severe cramps and pains in our bones. This morning I served about two tea-spoonfuls of rum to each person, and the allowance of bread and water, as usual. At noon the sun broke out, and revived every one. I found we were

in

1789.
MAY 19.
Tuesday
19.

Wednesday
20.

in latitude 14° 49′ S; longitude made 25° 46′ W; courſe S 88° W; diſtance 75 miles.

Thurſday, May the 21ſt. Freſh gales, and heavy ſhowers of rain. Wind E N E.

Our diſtreſſes were now very great, and we were ſo covered with rain and ſalt water, that we could ſcarcely ſee. Sleep, though we longed for it, afforded no comfort : for my own part, I almoſt lived without it: we ſuffered extreme cold, and every one dreaded the approach of night. About two o'clock in the morning we were overwhelmed with a deluge of rain. It fell ſo heavy that we were afraid it would fill the boat, and were obliged to bale with all our might. At dawn of day, I ſerved a large allowance of rum. Towards noon the rain abated and the ſun ſhone, but we were miſerably cold and wet, the ſea breaking ſo conſtantly over us, that, notwithſtanding the heavy rain, we had not been able to add to our ſtock of freſh water. The uſual allowance of one 25th of a pound of bread and water was ſerved at evening, morning, and noon. Latitude, by obſervation, 14° 29′ S, and longitude made, by account, from Tofoa, 27° 25′ W; courſe, ſince yeſterday noon, N 78° W, 99 miles. I now conſidered myſelf on a meridian with the eaſt part of New Guinea, and about 65 leagues diſtant from the coaſt of New Holland.

Friday, May the 22d. Strong gales from E S E to S S E, a high ſea, and dark diſmal night.

Our ſituation this day was extremely calamitous. We were obliged to take the courſe of the ſea, running right before it, and watching with the utmoſt care, as the leaſt error in the helm would in a moment have been our deſtruction. The ſea was continually breaking all over us; but, as we ſuffered not ſuch cold as when wet with the rain, I only ſerved the common allowance of bread and water.

At

At noon it **blew** very hard, and the foam of the fea kept running over our ftern and quarters; I however got propped up, and made an obfervation of the latitude, in 14° 17′ S; courfe N 85° W; diftance 130 miles; longitude made 29° 38′ weft.

· Saturday, May the 23d. Strong gales with very hard fqualls, and rain; wind S E, and S S E.

The mifery we fuffered this day exceeded the preceding. The night was dreadful. The fea flew over us with great force, and kept us baling with horror and anxiety. At dawn of day I found every one in a moft diftreffed condition, and I now began to fear that another fuch a night would put an end to the lives of feveral who feemed no longer able to fupport fuch fufferings. Every one complained of fevere pains in their bones; but thefe were alleviated, in fome degree, by an allowance of two tea-fpoonfuls of rum; after drinking which, having wrung our cloaths, and taken our breakfaft of bread and water, we became a little refrefhed.

Towards noon it became fair weather; but with very little abatement of the gale, and the fea remained equally high. With great difficulty I obferved the latitude to be 13° 44′ S; courfe N 74° W; diftance 116 miles fince yefterday; longitude made 31° 32′ W from Tofoa.

Sunday, May the 24th. Frefh gales and fine weather; wind S S E and S.

Towards the evening the weather looked much better, which rejoiced all hands, fo that they eat their fcanty allowance with more fatisfaction than for fome time paft. The night alfo was fair; but, being always wet with the fea, we fuffered much from the cold. A fine morning, I had the pleafure to fee, produce fome chearful countenances. Towards noon the weather improved, and, the firft time for 15

4

days

days paft, we found a little warmth from the fun. We ftripped, and hung our cloaths up to dry, which were by this time become fo thread-bare, that they would not keep out either wet or cold.

At noon I obferved in latitude 13° 33' S; longitude, by account, from Tofoa 33° 28' W; courfe N 84° W; diftance 114 miles. With the ufual allowance of bread and water for dinner, I ferved an ounce of pork to each perfon.

Monday
25. Monday, May the 25th. Frefh gales and fair weather. Wind S S E.

This afternoon we had many birds about us, which are never feen far from land, fuch as boobies and noddies.

About three o'clock the fea began to run fair, and we fhipped but little water, I therefore determined to know the exact quantity of bread I had left; and on examining found, according to my prefent iffues, fufficient for 29 days allowance. In the courfe of this time I hoped to be at Timor; but, as that was very uncertain, and perhaps after all we might be obliged to go to Java, I determined to pro-
Allowance
leffened. portion my iffues to fix weeks. I was apprehenfive that this would be ill received, and that it would require my utmoft refolution to enforce it; for, fmall as the quantity was which I intended to take away, for our future good, yet it might appear to my people like robbing them of life, and fome, who were lefs patient than their companions, I expected would very ill brook it. I however reprefented it fo effentially neceffary to guard againft delays in our voyage by contrary winds, or other caufes, promifing to enlarge upon the allowance as we got on, that it was readily agreed to. I therefore fixed, that every perfon fhould receive one 25th of a pound of bread for breakfaft, and one 25th of a pound for dinner; fo that by omitting the proportion for fupper, I had 43 days allowance.

At

At noon fome noddies came fo near to us, that one of them was caught by hand. This bird is about the fize of a fmall pigeon. I divided it, with its entrails, into 18 portions, and by the method of, Who fhall have this * ? it was diftributed with the allowance of bread and water for dinner, and eat up bones and all, with falt water for fauce. I obferved the latitude 13° 32′ S; longitude made 35° 19′ W; and courfe N 89° W; diftance 108 miles.

Tuefday, May the 26th. Frefh gales at S S E, and fine weather.

In the evening we faw feveral boobies flying fo near to us, that we caught one of them by hand. This bird is as large as a good duck; like the noddy, it has received its name from feamen, for fuffering itfelf to be caught on the mafts and yards of fhips. They are the moft prefumptive proofs of being in the neighbourhood of land of any fea-fowl we are acquainted with. I directed the bird to be killed for fupper, and the blood to be given to three of the people who were the moft diftreffed for want of food. The body, with the entrails, beak, and feet, I divided into 18 fhares, and with an allowance of bread, which I made a merit of granting, we made a good fupper, compared with our ufual fare.

In the morning we caught another booby, fo that Providence feemed to be relieving our wants in a very extraordinary manner. Towards noon we paffed a great many pieces of the branches of trees, fome of which appeared to have been no long time in the water. I had a good obfer-

---

* One perfon turns his back on the object that is to be divided. another then points feparately to the portions, at each of them afking aloud, " Who fhall have this ? " to which the firft anfwers by naming fomebody. This impartial method of divifion gives every man an equal chance of the beft fhare.

G   vation

vation for the latitude, and found my fituation to be in 13° 41′ S; my longitude, by account, from Tofoa, 37° 13′ W; courfe S 85° W, 112 miles. Every perfon was now overjoyed at the addition to their dinner, which I diftributed as I had done in the evening; giving the blood to thofe who were the moft in want of food.

To make our bread a little favoury we frequently dipped it in falt water; but for my own part I generally broke mine into fmall pieces, and eat it in my allowance of water, out of a cocoa-nut fhell, with a fpoon, economically avoiding to take too large a piece at a time, fo that I was as long at dinner as if it had been a much more plentiful meal.

Wednefday, May the 27th. Frefh breezes fouth-eafterly, and fine weather.

The weather was now ferene, but unhappily we found ourfelves unable to bear the fun's heat; many of us fuffering a languor and faintnefs, which made life indifferent. We were, however, fo fortunate as to catch two boobies to-day; their ftomachs contained feveral flying-fifh and fmall cuttlefifh, all of which I faved to be divided for dinner.

We paffed much drift wood, and faw many birds; I therefore did not hefitate to pronounce that we were near the reefs of New Holland, and affured every one I would make the coaft without delay, in the parallel we were in, and range the reef till I found an opening, through which we might get into fmooth water, and pick up fome fupplies. From my recollection of captain Cook's furvey of this coaft, I confidered the direction of it to be N W, and I was therefore fatisfied that, with the wind to the fouthward of E, I could always clear any dangers.

At noon I obferved in latitude 13° 26′ S; courfe fince yefterday N 82° W; diftance 109 miles; longitude made 39° 4′ W.

3   After

After writing my account, I divided the two birds with their entrails, and the contents of their maws, into 18 portions, and, as the prize was a very valuable one, it was divided as before, by calling out Who shall have this? so that to-day, with the allowance of a 25th of a pound of bread at breakfast, and another at dinner, with the proportion of water, I was happy to see that every person thought he had feasted.

Thursday, May the 28th. Fresh breezes and fair weather; wind ESE and E.

In the evening we saw a gannet; and the clouds remained so fixed in the west, that I had little doubt of our being near to New Holland; and every person, after taking his allowance of water for supper, began to divert himself with conversing on the probability of what we should find.

At one in the morning the person at the helm heard the sound of breakers, and I no sooner lifted up my head, than I saw them close under our lee, not more than a quarter of a mile distant from us. I immediately hauled on a wind to the NNE, and in ten minutes time we could neither see nor hear them.

I have already mentioned my reason for making New Holland so far to the southward; for I never doubted of numerous openings in the reef, through which I could have access to the shore: and, knowing the inclination of the coast to be to the NW, and the wind mostly to the southward of E, I could with ease range such a barrier of reefs till I should find a passage, which now became absolutely necessary, without a moment's loss of time. The idea of getting into smooth water, and finding refreshments, kept my people's spirits up: their joy was very great after we had got clear of the breakers, to which we

G 2

had

had been much nearer than I thought was poffible to be before we faw them.

In the morning, at day-light, I bore away again for the reefs, and faw them by nine o'clock. The fea broke furioufly over every part, and I had no fooner got near to them, than the wind came at E, fo that we could only lie along the line of the breakers, within which we faw the water fo fmooth, that every perfon already anticipated the heart-felt fatisfaction he would receive, as foon as we could get within them. But I now found we were embayed, for I could not lie clear with my fails, the wind having backed againft us, and the fea fet in fo heavy towards the reef that our fituation was become dangerous. We could effect but little with the oars, having fcarce ftrength to pull them ; and it was becoming every minute more and more probable that we fhould be obliged to attempt pufhing over the reef, in cafe we could not pull off. Even this I did not defpair of effecting with fuccefs, when happily we difcovered a break in the reef, about one mile from us, and at the fame time an ifland of a moderate height within it, nearly in the fame direction, bearing W ½ N. I entered the paffage with a ftrong ftream running to the weftward, and found it about a quarter of a mile broad, with every appearance of deep water.

On the outfide, the reef inclined to the N E for a few miles, and from thence to the N W ; on the fouth fide of the entrance, it inclined to the S S W as far as I could fee it ; and I conjecture that a fimilar paffage to this which we now entered, may be found near the breakers that I firft difcovered, which are 23 miles S of this channel.

I did not recollect what latitude Providential channel *

* Providential Channel is in 12° 34′ S, longitude 143° 33′ E.

lies

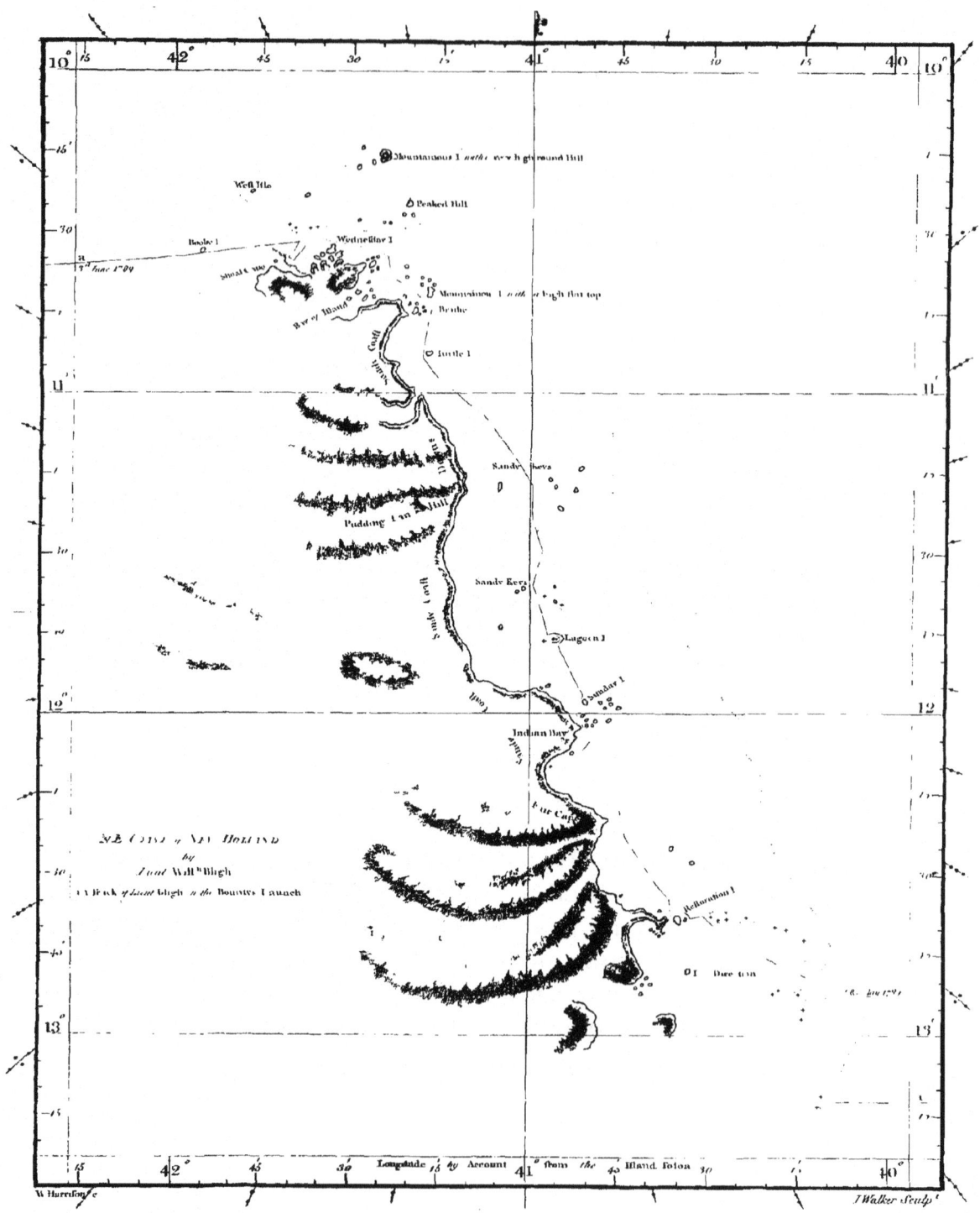

lies in, but I confidered it to be within a few miles of this, which is fituate in 12° 51′ S latitude.

Being now happily within the reefs, and in fmooth water, I endeavoured to keep near them to try for fifh; but the tide fet us to the N W; I therefore bore away in that direction, and, having promifed to land on the firft convenient fpot we could find, all our paft hardfhips feemed already to be forgotten.

At noon I had a good obfervation, by which our latitude was 12° 46 S, whence the foregoing fituations may be confidered as determined with fome exactnefs. The ifland firft feen bore W S W five leagues. This, which I have called the ifland Direction, will in fair weather always fhew the channel, from which it bears due W, and may be feen as foon as the reefs, from a fhip's maft-head: it lies in the latitude of 12° 51′ S. Thefe, however, are marks too fmall for a fhip to hit, unlefs it can hereafter be afcertained that paffages through the reef are numerous along the coaft, which I am inclined to think they are, and then there would be little rifk if the wind was not directly on the fhore.

My longitude, made by dead reckoning, from the ifland Tofoa to our paffage through the reef, is 40° 10′ W. Providential channel, I imagine, muft lie very nearly under the fame meridian with our paffage; by which it appears we had out-run our reckoning 1° 9′.

We now returned God thanks for his gracious protection, and with much content took our miferable allowance of a 25th of a pound of bread, and a quarter of a pint of water, for dinner.

Friday, May the 29th. Moderate breezes and fine weather, wind E S E.

As we advanced within the reefs, the coaft began to
fhew

shew itself very distinctly, with a variety of high and low land; some parts of which were covered with wood. In our way towards the shore we fell in with a point of a reef, which is connected with that towards the sea, and here I came to a grapnel, and tried to catch fish, but had no success. The island Direction now bore S three or four leagues. Two islands lay about four miles to the W by N, and appeared eligible for a resting-place, if nothing more; but on my approach to the first I found it only a heap of stones, and its size too inconsiderable to shelter the boat. I therefore proceeded to the next, which was close to it and towards the main, where, on the N W side, I found a bay and a fine sandy point to land at. Our distance was about a quarter of a mile from a projecting part of the main, bearing from S W by S, to N N W ¼ W. I now landed to examine if there were any signs of the natives being near us; but though I discovered some old fire-places, I saw nothing to alarm me for our situation during the night. Every one was anxious to find something to eat, and I soon heard that there were oysters on the rocks, for the tide was out; but it was nearly dark, and only a few could be gathered. I determined therefore to wait till the morning, to know how to proceed, and I consented that one half of us should sleep on shore, and the other in the boat. We would gladly have made a fire, but, as we could not accomplish it, we took our rest for the night, which happily was calm and undisturbed.

The dawn of day brought greater strength and spirits to us than I expected; for, notwithstanding every one was very weak, there appeared strength sufficient remaining to make me conceive the most favourable hopes of our being

able

able to furmount the difficulties we might yet have to en-
counter.

As foon as I faw that there were not any natives immediately near us, I fent out parties in fearch of fupplies,
while others were putting the boat in order, that I might
be ready to go to fea in cafe any unforefeen caufe might
make it neceffary. The firft object of this work, that demanded our attention, was the rudder: one of the gud-
geons had come out, in the courfe of the night, and was
loft. This, if it had happened at fea, would probably have
been the caufe of our perifhing, as the management of the
boat could not have been fo nicely preferved as thefe very
heavy feas required. I had often expreffed my fears of this
accident, and, that we might be prepared for it, had taken
the precaution to have grummets fixed on each quarter of
the boat for oars; but even our utmoft readinefs in ufing
them, I fear, would not have faved us. It appears, therefore, a providential circumftance, that it happened at this
place, and was in our power to remedy the defect; for by
great good luck we found a large ftaple in the boat that
anfwered the purpofe.

The parties were now returned, highly rejoiced at having found plenty of oyfters and frefh water. I alfo had
made a fire, by help of a fmall magnifying glafs, that I
always carried about me, to read off the divifions of my
fextants; and, what was ftill more fortunate, among the
few things which had been thrown into the boat and
faved, was a piece of brimftone and a tinder-box, fo that I
fecured fire for the future.

One of my people had been fo provident as to bring
away with him a copper pot: it was by being in poffeffion
of this article that I was enabled to make a proper ufe of
the

the fupply we found, for, with a mixture of bread and a little pork, I made a ftew that might have been relifhed by people of more delicate appetites, of which each perfon received a full pint.

The general complaints of difeafe among us, were a dizzinefs in the head, great weaknefs of the joints, and violent tenefmus, moft of us having had no evacuation by ftool fince we left the fhip. I had conftantly a fevere pain at my ftomach; but none of our complaints were alarming; on the contrary, every one retained marks of ftrength, that, with a mind poffeffed of any fortitude, could bear more fatigue than I hoped we had to undergo in our voyage to Timor.

As I would not allow the people to expofe themfelves to the heat of the fun, it being near noon, every one took his allotment of earth, fhaded by the bufhes, for a fhort fleep.

The oyfters we found grew fo faft to the rocks that it was with difficulty they could be broke off, and at laft we difcovered it to be the moft expeditious way to open them where they were found. They were very fizeable, and well tafted, and gave us great relief. To add to this happy circumftance, in the hollow of the land there grew fome wire grafs, which indicated a moift fituation. On forcing a ftick, about three feet long, into the ground, we found water, and with little trouble dug a well, which produced as much as we were in need of. It was very good, but I could not determine if it was a fpring or not. Our wants made it not neceffary to make the well deep, for it flowed as faft as we emptied it; which, as the foil was apparently too loofe to retain water from the rains, renders it probable to be a fpring. It lies about 200 yards to the SE of a point in the SW part of the ifland.

I found

1789.
MAY 29.

I found evident figns of the natives reforting to this ifland; for, befides fire-places, I faw two miferable wig-wams, having only one fide loofely covered. We found a pointed ftick, about three feet long, with a flit in the end of it, to fling ftones with, the fame as the natives of Van Diemen's land ufe.

The track of fome animal was very difcernible, and Mr. Nelfon agreed with me that it was the Kanguroo; but how thefe animals can get from the main I know not, unlefs brought over by the natives to breed, that they may take them with more eafe, and render a fupply of food certain to them; as on the continent the catching of them may be precarious, or attended with great trouble, in fo large an extent of country.

The ifland may be about two miles in circuit; it is a high lump of rocks and ftones covered with wood; but the trees are fmall, the foil, which is very indifferent and fandy, being barely fufficient to produce them. The trees that came within our knowledge were the manchineal and a fpecies of purow: alfo fome palm-trees, the tops of which we cut down, and the foft interior part or heart of them was fo palatable that it made a good addition to our mefs. Mr. Nelfon difcovered fome fern-roots, which I thought might be good roafted, as a fubftitute for bread, but it proved a very poor one: it however was very good in its natural ftate to allay thirft, and on that account I directed a quantity to be collected to take into the boat. Many pieces of cocoa-nut fhells and hufk were found about the fhore, but we could find no cocoa-nut trees, neither did I fee any like them on the main.

I had cautioned every one not to touch any kind of berry or fruit that they might find; yet they were no

H.   fooner sooner out of my fight than they began to make free with three different kinds, that grew all over the ifland, eating without any referve. The fymptoms of having eaten too much, began at laft to frighten fome of them; but on queftioning others, who had taken a more moderate allowance, their minds were a little quieted. The others, however, became equally alarmed in their turn, dreading that fuch fymptoms would come on, and that they were all poifoned, fo that they regarded each other with the ftrongeft marks of apprehenfion, uncertain what would be the iffue of their imprudence. Happily the fruit proved wholefome and good. One fort grew on a fmall delicate kind of vine; they were the fize of a large goofeberry, and very like in fubftance, but had only a fweet tafte; the fkin was a pale red, ftreaked with yellow the long way of the fruit: it was pleafant and agreeable. Another kind grew on bufhes, like that which is called the fea-fide grape in the Weft Indies; but the fruit was very different, and more like elder-berries, growing in clufters in the fame manner. The third fort was a black berry, not in fuch plenty as the others, and refembled a bullace, or large kind of floe, both in fize and tafte. Seeing thefe fruits eaten by the birds made me confider them fit for ufe, and thofe who had already tried the experiment, not finding any bad effect, made it a certainty that we might eat of them without danger.

Wild pigeons, parrots, and other birds, were about the fummit of the ifland, but, as I had no fire-arms, relief of that kind was not to be expected, unlefs I met with fome unfrequented fpot where we might take them with our hands.

On the fouth fide of the ifland, and about half a mile

2

from

from the well, a small run of water was found; but, as its source was not traced, I know nothing more of it.

The shore of this island is very rocky, except the part we landed at, and here I picked up many pieces of pumice-stone. On the part of the main next to us were several sandy bays, but at low-water they became an extensive rocky flat. The country had rather a barren appearance, except in a few places where it was covered with wood. A remarkable range of rocks lay a few miles to the S W, or a high peaked hill terminated the coast towards the sea, with other high lands and islands to the southward. A high fair cape showed the direction of the coast to the N W, about seven leagues, and two small isles lay three or four leagues to the northward.

I saw a few bees or wasps, several lizards, and the black-berry bushes were full of ants nests, webbed as a spider's, but so close and compact as not to admit the rain.

A trunk of a tree, about 50 feet long, lay on the beach; from whence I conclude a heavy sea runs in here with the northerly winds.

This being the day of the restoration of king Charles the Second, and the name not being inapplicable to our present situation (for we were restored to fresh life and strength), I named this Restoration Island; for I thought it probable that captain Cook might not have taken notice of it. The other names I have presumed to give the different parts of the coast, will be only to show my route a little more distinctly.

At noon I found the latitude of the island to be 12° 39′ S; our course having been N 66° W; distance 18 miles from yesterday noon.

Saturday, May the 30th. Very fine weather, and ESE winds.

winds. This afternoon I fent parties out again to gather oyfters, with which and fome of the inner part of the palm-top, we made another good ftew for fupper, each perfon receiving a full pint and a half; but I refufed bread to this meal, for I confidered our wants might yet be very great, and as fuch I reprefented the neceffity of faving our principal fupport whenever it was in our power.

At night we again divided, and one half of us flept on fhore by a good fire. In the morning I difcovered a vifible alteration in every one for the better, and I fent them away again to gather oyfters. I had now only two pounds of pork left. This article, which I could not keep under lock and key as I did the bread, had been pilfered by fome inconfiderate perfon, but every one moft folemnly denied it; I therefore refolved to put it out of their power for the future, by fharing what remained for our dinner. While the party was out getting oyfters, I got the boat in readinefs for fea, and filled all our water veffels, which amounted to nearly 60 gallons.

The party being returned, dinner was foon ready, and every one had as good an allowance as they had for fupper; for with the pork I gave an allowance of bread; and I was determined forthwith to pufh on. As it was not yet noon, I told every one that an exertion fhould be made to gather as many oyfters as poffible for a fea ftore, as I was determined to fail in the afternoon.

At noon I again obferved the latitude 12° 39′ S; it was then high-water, the tide had rifen three feet, but I could not be certain which way the flood came from. I deduce the time of high-water at full and change to be ten minutes paft feven in the morning.

Sunday, May the 31ft. Early in the afternoon, the people

ple

ple returned with the few oysters they had time to pick up, and every thing was put into the boat. I then examined the quantity of bread remaining, and found 38 days allowance, according to the last mode of issuing a 25th of a pound at breakfast and at dinner.

Fair weather, and moderate breezes at E S E and S E.

Being all ready for sea, I directed every person to attend prayers, and by four o'clock we were preparing to embark; when twenty natives appeared, running and holloaing to us, on the opposite shore. They were armed with a spear or lance, and a short weapon which they carried in their left hand: they made signs for us to come to them. On the top of the hills we saw the heads of many more; whether these were their wives and children, or others who waited for our landing, until which they meant not to show themselves, lest we might be intimidated, I cannot say; but, as I found we were discovered to be on the coast, I thought it prudent to make the best of my way, for fear of canoes; though, from the accounts of captain Cook, the chance was that there were very few or none of any consequence. I passed these people as near as I could, which was within a quarter of a mile; they were naked, and apparently black, and their hair or wool bushy and short.

I directed my course within two small islands that lie to the north of Restoration Island, passing between them and the main land, towards Fair Cape, with a strong tide in my favour; so that I was abreast of it by eight o'clock. The coast I had passed was high and woody. As I could see no land without Fair Cape, I concluded that the coast inclined to the N W and W N W, which was agreeable to my recollection of captain Cook's survey. I therefore steered more towards the W; but by eleven o'clock at night I found
myself

myfelf miftaken: for we met with low land, which inclined to the N E; fo that at three o'clock in the morning I found we were embayed, which obliged us to ftand back to the fouthward.

At day-break I was exceedingly furprifed to find the appearance of the country all changed, as if in the courfe of the night I had been tranfported to another part of the world; for we had now a miferable low fandy coaft in view, with very little verdure, or any thing to indicate that it was at all habitable to a human being, if I except fome patches of fmall trees or brufh-wood.

I had many fmall iflands in view to the N E, about fix miles diftant. The E part of the main bore N four miles, and Fair Cape S S E five or fix leagues. I took the channel between the neareft ifland and the main land, about one mile apart, leaving all the iflands on the ftarboard fide. Some of thefe were very pretty fpots, covered with wood, and well fituated for fifhing: large fhoals of fifh were about us, but we could not catch any. As I was paffing this ftrait we faw another party of Indians, feven in number, running towards us, fhouting and making figns for us to land. Some of them waved green branches of the bufhes which were near them, as a fign of friendfhip; but there were fome of their other motions lefs friendly. A larger party we faw a little farther off, and coming towards us. I therefore determined not to land, though I wifhed much to have had fome intercourfe with thefe people; for which purpofe I beckoned to them to come near to me, and laid the boat clofe to the rocks; but not one would come within 200 yards of us. They were armed in the fame manner as thofe I had feen from Reftoration Ifland, were ftark naked, and appeared to be jet black, with fhort bufhy

hair

hair or wool, and in every respect the same people. An
island of good height now bore N ½ W, four miles from
us, at which I resolved to see what could be got, and from
thence to take a look at the coast. At this isle I landed
about eight o'clock in the morning. The shore was rocky,
with some sandy beaches within the rocks: the water,
however, was smooth, and I landed without difficulty.
I sent two parties out, one to the northward, and the
other to the southward, to seek for supplies, and others
I ordered to stay by the boat. On this occasion their
fatigue and weakness so far got the better of their sense
of duty, that some of them began to mutter who had
done most, and declared they would rather be without
their dinner than go in search of it. One person, in
particular, went so far as to tell me, with a mutinous
look, he was as good a man as myself. It was not
possible for me to judge where this might have an end, if
not stopped in time; I therefore determined to strike a
final blow at it, and either to preserve my command, or
die in the attempt: and, seizing a cutlass, I ordered him
to take hold of another and defend himself; on which he
called out I was going to kill him, and began to make
concessions. I did not allow this to interfere further with
the harmony of the boat's crew, and every thing soon became quiet.

The parties continued collecting what could be found,
which consisted of some fine oysters and clams, and a few
small dog-fish that were caught in the holes of the rocks.
We also found about two tons of rain-water in the hollow of
the rocks, on the north part of the island, so that of this es-
sential article we were again so happy as not to be in want.

After regulating the mode of proceeding, I set off for the
highest

1789.
MAY 31.

higheſt part of the iſland, to ſee and conſider of my route for the night. To my ſurpriſe I could ſee no more of the main than I did from below, it extending only from S ½ E, four miles, to W by N, about three leagues, full of ſand-hills. Beſides the iſles to the E S E and ſouth, that I had ſeen before, I could only diſcover a ſmall key N W by N. As this was conſiderably farther from the main than where I was at preſent, I reſolved to get there by night, it being a more ſecure reſting-place; for I was here open to an attack, if the Indians had canoes, as they undoubtedly obſerved my landing. My mind being made up on this point, I returned, taking a particular look at the ſpot I was on, which I found only to produce a few buſhes and coarſe graſs, and the extent of the whole not two miles in circuit. On the north ſide, in a ſandy bay, I ſaw an old canoe, about 33 feet long, lying bottom upwards, and half buried in the beach. It was made of three pieces, the bottom entire, to which the ſides were ſewed in the common way. It had a ſharp projecting prow rudely carved, in reſemblance of the head of a fiſh; the extreme breadth was about three feet, and I imagine it was capable of carrying 20 men.

At noon the parties were all returned, but had found difficulty in gathering the oyſters, from their cloſe adherence to the rocks, and the clams were ſcarce: I therefore ſaw, that it would be of little uſe to remain longer in this place, as we ſhould not be able to collect more than we could eat; nor could any tolerable ſea-ſtore be expected, unleſs we fell in with a greater plenty. I named this Sunday Iſland: it lies N by W ¼ W from Reſtoration Iſland; the latitude, by a good obſervation, 11° 58′ S.

Monday, June the 1ſt. Freſh breezes and fair weather, ending with a freſh gale. Wind S E by S.

At

At two o'clock in the afternoon, we dined; each perfon having a full pint and a half of ftewed oyfters and clams, thickened with fmall beans, which Mr. Nelfon informed us were a fpecies of Dolichos. Having eaten heartily, and taken the water we were in want of, I only waited to determine the time of high-water, which I found to be at three o'clock, and the rife of the tide about five feet. According to this it is high-water on the full and change at 19 minutes paft 9 in the morning; but here I obferved the flood to come from the fouthward, though at Reftoration Ifland, I thought it came from the northward. I think captain Cook mentions that he found great irregularity in the fet of the flood on this coaft.

I now failed for the key which I had feen in the N W by N, giving the name of Sunday Ifland to the place I left; we arrived juft at dark, but found it fo furrounded by a reef of rocks, that I could not land without danger of ftaving the boat; and on that account I came to a grapnel for the night.

At dawn of day we got on fhore, and tracked the boat into fhelter; for the wind blowing frefh without, and the ground being rocky, I was afraid to truft her at a grapnel, left fhe might be blown to fea: I was, therefore, obliged to let her ground in the courfe of the ebb. From appearances, I expected that if we remained till night we fhould meet with turtle, as we had already difcovered recent tracks of them. Innumerable birds of the noddy kind made this ifland their refting-place; fo that I had reafon to flatter myfelf with hopes of getting fupplies in greater abundance than it had hitherto been in my power. The fituation was at leaft four leagues diftant from the main. We were on the north-wefternmoft of four

I   fmall

small keys, which were surrounded by a reef of rocks connected by sand-banks, except between the two northernmost; and there likewise it was dry at low water; the whole forming a lagoon island, into which the tide flowed: at this entrance I kept the boat.

As usual, I sent parties away in search of supplies, but, to our great disappointment, we could only get a few clams and some dolichos : with these, and the oysters we had brought from Sunday Island, I made up a mess for dinner, with an addition of a small quantity of bread.

Towards noon, Mr. Nelson, and his party, who had been to the easternmost key, returned; but himself in such a weak condition, that he was obliged to be supported by two men. His complaint was a violent heat in his bowels, a loss of sight, much drought, and an inability to walk. This I found was occasioned by his being unable to support the heat of the sun, and that, when he was fatigued and faint, instead of retiring into the shade to rest, he had continued to do more than his strength was equal to. It was a great satisfaction to me to find, that he had no fever; and it was now that the little wine, which I had so carefully saved, became of real use. I gave it in very small quantities, with some small pieces of bread soaked in it; and, having pulled off his cloaths, and laid him under some shady bushes, he began to recover. The boatswain and carpenter also were ill, and complained of head-ach, and sickness of the stomach; others, who had not had any evacuation by stool, became shockingly distressed with the tenesmus; so that there were but few without complaints. An idea now prevailed, that their illness was occasioned by eating the dolichos, and some were so much alarmed that they thought themselves poisoned. Myself, however,

however, and fome others, who had eaten of them, were yet very well; but the truth was, that all thofe who were complaining, except Mr. Nelfon, had gorged themfelves with a large quantity of raw beans, and Mr. Nelfon informed me, that they were conftantly teazing him, whenever a berry was found, to know if it was good to eat; fo that it would not have been furpiizing if many of them had been really poifoned.

Our dinner was not fo well relifhed as at Sunday Ifland, becaufe we had mixed the dolichos with our ftew. The oyfters and foup, however, were eaten by every one, except Mr. Nelfon, whom I fed with a few fmall pieces of bread foaked in half a glafs of wine, and he continued to mend.

In my walk round the ifland, I found feveral cocoa-nut fhells, the remains of an old wigwam, and the backs of two turtle, but no fign of any quadruped. One of my people found three fea-fowl's eggs.

As is common on fuch fpots, the foil is little other than fand, yet it produced fmall toa-trees, and fome others, that we were not acquainted with. There were fifh in the lagoon, but we could not catch any. As our wants, therefore, were not likely to be fupplied here, not even with water for our daily expence, I determined to fail in the morning, after trying our fuccefs in the night for turtle and birds. A quiet night's reft alfo, I conceived, would be of effential fervice to thofe who were unwell.

From the wigwam and turtle-fhell being found, it is certain that the natives fometimes refort to this place, and have canoes: but I did not apprehend that we ran any rifk by remaining here. I directed our fire, however, to be made in the thicket, that we might not be difcovered in the night.

I 2   At

At noon, I obferved the latitude of this ifland to be 11° 47′ S. The main land extended towards the N W, and was full of white fand-hills: another fmall ifland lay within us, bearing W by N ¼ N, three leagues diftant. My fituation being very low, I could fee nothing of the reef towards the fea.

Tuefday, June the 2d. The firft part of this day we had fome light fhowers of rain; the latter part was fair, wind from the S E, blowing frefh.

Reft was now fo much wanted, that the afternoon was advantageoufly fpent in fleep. There were, however, a few not difpofed to it, and thofe I employed in dreffing fome clams to take with us for the next day's dinner; others we cut up in flices to dry, which I knew was the moft valuable fupply we could find here. But, contrary to our expectation, they were very fcarce.

Towards evening, I cautioned every one againft making too large a fire, or fuffering it after dark to blaze up. Mr. Samuel and Mr. Peckover had the fuperintendence of this bufinefs, while I was ftrolling about the beach to obferve if I thought it could be feen from the main. I was juft fatif-fied that it could not, when on a fudden the ifland appeared all in a blaze, that might have been feen at a much more confiderable diftance. I ran to learn the caufe, and found it was occafioned by the imprudence and obftinacy of one of the party, who, in my abfence, had infifted on having a fire to himfelf; in making which the flames caught the neighbouring grafs and rapidly fpread. This mif-conduct might have produced very ferious confequences, by difcovering our fituation to the natives; for, if they had attacked us, we muft inevitably have fallen a facrifice, as

we

we had neither arms nor ftrength to oppofe an enemy. Thus the relief which I expected from a little fleep was totally loft, and I anxioufly waited for the flowing of the tide, that we might proceed to fea.

I found it high-water at half paft five this evening, whence I deduce the time, on the full and change of the moon, to be 58′ paft 10 in the morning : the rife is nearly five feet. I could not obferve the fet of the flood ; but imagine it comes from the fouthward, and that I have been miftaken at Reftoration Ifland, as I find the time of high-water gradually later as we advance to the north-ward.

At Reftoration Ifland, high water, full and change, 7ʰ 10ᶜ
Sunday Ifland, - - - - - - 9 19
Here, - - - - - - - 10 58

After eight o'clock, Mr. Samuel and Mr. Peckover went out to watch for turtle, and three men went to the eaft key to endeavour to catch birds. All the others complaining of being fick, took their reft, except Mr. Hayward and Mr. Elphinfton, who I directed to keep watch. About midnight the bird party returned, with only twelve noddies, a bird I have already defcribed to be about the fize of a pigeon : but if it had not been for the folly and obftinacy of one of the party, who feparated from the other two, and difturbed the birds, they might have caught a great number. I was fo much provoked at my plans being thus defeated, that I gave the offender * a good beating. I now went in fearch of the turtling party, who had taken great pains, but without fuccefs. This, however, did not furprife me, as it was not to be expected that

* Robert Lamb —This man, when he came to Java, acknowledged he had eaten nine birds on the key, after he feparated from the other two.

turtle

turtle would come near us after the noise which was made at the beginning of the evening in extinguishing the fire. I therefore defired them to come back, but they requefted to ftay a little longer, as they ftill hoped to find fome before day-light: they, however, returned by three o'clock, without any reward for their labour.

The birds we half dreffed, which, with a few clams, made the whole of the fupply procured here. I tied up a few gilt buttons and fome pieces of iron to a tree, for any of the natives that might come after us; and, happily finding my invalids much better for their night's reft, I got every one into the boat, and departed by dawn of day. Wind at S E; courfe to the N by W.

We had fcarcely ran two leagues to the northward, when the fea fuddenly became rough, which not having experienced fince we were within the reefs, I concluded to be occafioned by an open channel to the ocean. Soon afterwards we met with a large fhoal, on which were two fandy keys; between thefe and two others, four miles to the weft, I paffed on to the northward, the fea ftill continuing to be rough.

Towards noon, I fell in with fix other keys, moft of which produced fome fmall trees and brufh-wood. Thefe formed a pleafing contraft with the main land we had paffed, which was full of fand-hills. The country continued hilly, and the northernmoft land, the fame which we faw from the lagoon ifland, appeared like downs, floping towards the fea. To the fouthward of this is a flat-topped hill, which, on account of its fhape, I called Pudding-pan hill, and a little to the northward two other hills, which we called the Paps; and here was a fmall tract of country

5   without

without fand, the eaftern part of which forms a cape, whence the coaft inclines to the N W by N.

At noon I obferved in the latitude of 11° 18′ S, the cape bearing W, diftant ten miles. Five fmall keys bore from N E to S E, the neareft of them about two miles diftant, and a low fandy key between us and the cape bore W, diftant four miles. My courfe from the Lagoon Ifland N ½ W, diftant 30 miles.

I am forry it was not in my power to obtain a fufficient knowledge of the depth of water; for in our fituation nothing could be undertaken that might have occafioned delay. It may however be underftood, that, to the beft of my judgment, from appearances, a fhip may pafs wherever I have omitted to reprefent danger.

I divided fix birds, and iffued one 25th of a pound of bread, with half a pint of water, to each perfon for dinner, and I gave half a glafs of wine to Mr. Nelfon, who was now fo far recovered as to require no other indulgence.

The gunner, when he left the fhip, brought his watch with him, by which we had regulated our time till to-day, when unfortunately it ftopped; fo that noon, fun-rife, and fun-fet, are the only parts of the 24 hours of which I can fpeak with certainty, as to time.

Wednefday, June the 3d. Frefh gales S S E and S E, and fair weather. As we ftood to the N by W this afternoon, we found more fea, which I attributed to our receiving lefs fhelter from the reefs to the eaftward: it is probable they do not extend fo far to the N as this; at leaft, it may be concluded that there is not a continued barrier to prevent fhipping having accefs to the fhore. I obferved that the ftream fet to the N W, which I confidered to be the flood; in fome places along the coaft, we faw patches of
wood.

wood. At five o'clock, steering to the N W, we passed a large and fair inlet, into which, I imagine, is a safe and commodious entrance; it lies in latitude 11°S: about three leagues to the northward of this is an island, at which we arrived about sun-set, and took shelter for the night under a sandy point, which was the only part we could land at: I was therefore under the necessity to put up with rather a wild situation, and slept in the boat. Nevertheless I sent a party away to see what could be got, but they returned without any success. They saw a great number of turtle bones and shells, where the natives had been feasting, and their last visit seemed to be of late date. The island was covered with wood, but in other respects a lump of rocks. We lay at a grapnel until day-light, with a very fresh gale and cloudy weather. The main bore from S E by S to N N W ½ W, three leagues; and a mountainous island, with a flat top, N by W, four or five leagues: several others were between it and the main. The spot we were on, which I call Turtle Island, lies in latitude, by account, 10° 52′ S, and 42 miles W from Restoration Island. Abreast of it the coast has the appearance of a sandy desert, but improves about three leagues farther to the northward, where it terminates in a point, near to which is a number of small islands. I sailed between these islands, where I found no bottom at twelve fathoms; the high mountainous island with a flat top, and four rocks to the S E of it, that I call the Brothers, being on my starboard hand. Soon after, an extensive opening appeared in the main land, with a number of high islands in it. I called this the Bay of Islands. We continued steering to the N W. Several islands and keys lay to the northward. The most northerly island was mountainous, having on it

a very

a very high round hill; and a ſmaller was remarkable for a ſingle peaked hill.

The coaſt to the northward and weſtward of the Bay of Iſlands had a very different appearance from that to the ſouthward. It was high and woody, with many iſlands cloſe to it, and had a very broken appearance. Among theſe iſlands are fine bays, and convenient places for ſhipping. The northernmoſt I call Wedneſday Iſland: to the N W of this we fell in with a large reef, which I believe joins a number of keys that were in ſight from the N W to the E N E. We now ſtood to the S W half a league, when it was noon, and I had a good obſervation of the latitude in 10° 31′ S. Wedneſday Iſland bore E by S five miles; the weſternmoſt land S W two or three leagues; the iſlands to the northward, from N W by W four or five leagues, to N E ſix leagues; and the reef from W to N E, diſtant one mile. I now aſſured every one that we ſhould be clear of New Holland in the afternoon.

It is impoſſible for me to ſay how far this reef may extend. It may be a continuation, or a detached part of the range of ſhoals that ſurround the coaſt: but be that as it may, I conſider the mountainous iſlands as ſeparate from the ſhoals; and have no doubt that near them may be found good paſſages for ſhips. But I rather recommend to thoſe who are to paſs this ſtrait from the eaſtward, to take their direction from the coaſt of New Guinea: yet, I likewiſe think that a ſhip coming from the ſouthward, will find a fair ſtrait in the latitude of 10° S. I much wiſhed to have aſcertained this point; but in our diſtreſsful ſituation, any increaſe of fatigue, or loſs of time, might have been attended with the moſt fatal conſequences. I therefore determined to paſs on without delay.

K

As

As an addition to our dinner of bread and water, I ſerved to each perſon ſix oyſters.

Thurſday, June the 4th.   A freſh gale at S E, and fair weather.

At two o'clock, as we were ſteering to the S W, towards the weſteinmoſt part of the land in fight, we fell in with ſome large ſand-banks that run off from the coaſt.   We were therefore obliged to ſteer to the northward again, and, having got round them, I directed my courſe to the W.

At four o'clock, the weſternmoſt of the iſlands to the northward bore N four leagues; Wedneſday iſland E by N five leagues; and Shoal Cape S E by E two leagues.   A ſmall iſland was now ſeen bearing W, at which I arrived before dark, and found that it was only a rock, where boobies reſort, for which reaſon I called it Booby Iſland. A ſmall key alſo lies cloſe to the W part of the coaſt, which I have called Shoal Cape.   Here terminated the rocks and ſhoals of the N part of New Holland, for, except Booby Iſland, we could ſee no land to the weſtward of S, after three o'clock this afternoon.

I find that Booby Iſland was ſeen by Captain Cook, and, by a remarkable coincidence of ideas, received from him the ſame name; but I cannot with certainty reconcile the ſituation of many parts of the coaſt that I have ſeen, to his ſurvey.   I aſcribe this to the very different form in which land appears, when ſeen from the unequal heights of a ſhip and a boat.   The chart I have given, is by no means meant to ſuperſede that made by Captain Cook, who had better opportunities than I had, and was in every reſpect properly provided for ſurveying.   The intention of mine is chiefly to render the narrative more intelligible, and to

ſhew

fhew in what manner the coaft appeared to me from an open boat. I have little doubt that the opening, which I named the Bay of Iflands, is Endeavour Straits; and that our track was to the northward of Prince of Wales's Ifles. Perhaps, by thofe who fhall hereafter navigate thefe feas, more advantage may be derived from the poffeffion of both our charts, than from either fingly.

At eight o'clock in the evening, we once more launched into the open ocean. Miferable as our fituation was in every refpect, I was fecretly furprifed to fee that it did not appear to affect any one fo ftrongly as myfelf; on the contrary, it feemed as if they had embarked on a voyage to Timor, in a veffel fufficiently calculated for fafety and convenience. So much confidence gave me great pleafure, and I may affert that to this caufe their prefervation is chiefly to be attributed; for if any one of them had defpaired, he would moft probably have died before we reached New Holland.

I now gave every one hopes that eight or ten days might bring us to a land of fafety; and, after praying to God for a continuance of his moft gracious protection, I ferved an allowance of water for fupper, and kept my courfe to the W S W, to counteract the foutherly winds, in cafe they fhould blow ftrong.

We had been juft fix days on the coaft of New Holland, in the courfe of which we found oyfters, a few clams, fome birds, and water. But perhaps a benefit nearly equal to this we received from not having fatigue in the boat, and enjoying good reft at night. Thefe advantages certainly preferved our lives; for, fmall as the fupply was, I am very fenfible how much it relieved our diftreffes.

K 2   About

About this time nature would have funk under the extremes of hunger and fatigue. Some would have ceafed to ftruggle for a life that only promifed wretchednefs and mifery; while others, though poffeffed of more bodily ftrength, muft foon have followed their unfortunate companions. Even in our prefent fituation, we were moft wretched fpectacles; yet our fortitude and fpirit remained; every one being encouraged by the hopes of a fpeedy termination to his mifery.

For my own part, wonderful as it may appear, I felt neither extreme hunger nor thirft. My allowance contented me, knowing I could have no more.

I ferved one 25th of a pound of bread, and an allowance of water, for breakfaft, and the fame for dinner, with an addition of fix oyfters to each perfon. At noon, latitude obferved 10° 48′ S; courfe fince yefterday noon S 81 W; diftance 111 miles; longitude, by account, from Shoal Cape 1° 45′ W.

Friday, June the 5th. Fair weather with fome fhowers, and a ftrong trade wind at E S E.

This day we faw a number of water-fnakes, that were ringed yellow and black, and towards noon we paffed a great deal of rock-weed. Though the weather was fair, we were conftantly fhipping water, and two men always employed to bale the boat.

At noon I obferved in latitude 10° 45′ S; our courfe fince yefterday W ¼ N, 108 miles; longitude made 3° 35′ W. Served one 25th of a pound of bread, and a quarter of a pint of water for breakfaft; the fame for dinner, with an addition of fix oyfters; for fupper water only.

Saturday, June the 6th. Fair weather, with fome fhowers, and a frefh gale at S E and E S E. Conftantly fhipping water and baling.

In

In the evening a few boobies came about us, one of which I caught with my hand. The blood was divided among three of the men who were weakeſt, but the bird I ordered to be kept for our dinner the next day. Served a quarter of a pint of water for ſupper, and to ſome, who were moſt in need, half a pint.

In the courſe of the night we ſuffered much cold and ſhiverings. At day-light, I found that ſome of the clams, which had been hung up to dry for ſea-ſtore, were ſtolen; but every one moſt ſolemnly denied having any knowledge of it. This forenoon we ſaw a gannet, a ſand-lark, and ſome water-ſnakes, which in general were from two to three feet long.

Served the uſual allowance of bread and water for breakfaſt, and the ſame for dinner, with the bird, which I diſtributed in the uſual way, of Who ſhall have this? I determined to make Timor about the latitude of 9° 30′ S, or 10° S. At noon I obſerved the latitude to be 10° 19′ S; courſe N 77° W; diſtance 117 miles; longitude made from the Shoal Cape, the north part of New Holland, 5° 31′ W.

Sunday, June the 7th. Freſh gales and fair weather till eight in the evening. The remaining part of the 24 hours ſqually, with much wind at S S E and E S E, and a high ſea, ſo that we were conſtantly wet and baling.

In the afternoon, I took an opportunity of examining again into our ſtore of bread, and found remaining 19 days allowance, at my former rate of ſerving one 25th of a pound three times a day: therefore, as I ſaw every proſpect of a quick paſſage, I again ventured to grant an allowance for ſupper, agreeable to my promiſe at the time it was diſcontinued.

We paſſed the night miſerably wet and cold, and in the morning

morning I heard heavy complaints of our deplorable situation. The sea was high and breaking over us. I could only afford the allowance of bread and water for breakfast; but for dinner I gave out an ounce of dried clams to each person, which was all that remained.

At noon I altered the course to the W N W, to keep more from the sea while it blew so strong. Latitude observed 9° 31′ S; course N 57° W; distance 88 miles; longitude made 6° 46′ W.

Monday
8

Monday, June the 8th. Fresh gales and squally weather, with some showers of rain. Wind E and E S E.

This day the sea ran very high, and we were continually wet, suffering much cold in the night. I now remarked that Mr. Ledward, the surgeon, and Lawrence Lebogue, an old hardy seaman, were giving way very fast. I could only assist them by a tea-spoonful or two of wine, which I had carefully saved, expecting such a melancholy necessity. Among most of the others I observed more than a common inclination to sleep, which seemed to indicate that nature was almost exhausted.

Served the usual allowance of bread and water at supper, breakfast, and dinner. Saw several gannets.

At noon I observed in 8° 45′ S; course W N W ¼ W, 106 miles; longitude made 8° 23′ W.

Tuesday
9.

Tuesday, June the 9th. Wind S E. The weather being moderate, I steered W by S.

At four in the afternoon we caught a small dolphin, the first relief of the kind we obtained. I issued about two ounces to each person, including the offals, and saved the remainder for dinner the next day. Towards evening the wind freshened, and it blew strong all night, so that we shipped much water, and suffered greatly from the wet and cold.

At

At day-light, as ufual, I heard much complaining, which my own feelings convinced me was too well founded. I gave the furgeon and Lebogue a little wine, but I could give no farther relief, than affurances that a very few days longer, at our prefent fine rate of failing, would bring us to Timor.

Gannets, boobies, men of war and tropic birds, were conftantly about us. Served the ufual allowance of bread and water, and at noon dined on the remains of the dolphin, which amounted to about an ounce per man. I obferved the latitude to be 9° 9′ S; longitude made 10° 8′ W; courfe fince yefterday noon S 76° W; diftance 107 miles.

Wednefday, June the 10th. Wind E S E. Frefh gales and fair weather, but a continuance of much fea, which, by breaking almoft conftantly over the boat, made us miferably wet, and we had much cold to endure in the night.

This afternoon I fuffered great ficknefs from the oily nature of part of the ftomach of the fifh, which had fallen to my fhare at dinner. At fun-fet I ferved an allowance of bread and water for fupper. In the morning, after a very bad night, I could fee an alteration for the worfe in more than half my people. The ufual allowance was ferved for breakfaft and dinner. At noon I found our fituation to be in latitude 9° 16′ S; longitude from the north part of New Holland 12° 1 W; courfe fince yefterday noon W ½ S, diftance 111 miles.

Thurfday, June the 11th. Frefh gales and fair weather. Wind S E and S S E.

Birds and rock-weed fhowed that we were not far from land; but I expected fuch figns muft be here, as there are many iflands between the eaft part of Timor and New Guinea. I however hoped to fall in with Timor every hour,

4

hour, for I had great apprehenfions that fome of my people could not hold out. An extreme weaknefs, fwelled
legs, hollow and ghaftly countenances, great propenfity to
fleep, with an apparent debility of underftanding, feemed
to me melancholy prefages of their approaching diffolution.
The furgeon and Lebogue, in particular, were moft miferable objects. I occafionally gave them a few tea-fpoonfuls
of wine, out of the little I had faved for this dreadful
ftage, which no doubt greatly helped to fupport them.

For my own part, a great fhare of fpirits, with the hopes
of being able to accomplifh the voyage, feemed to be my
principal fupport; but the boatfwain very innocently told
me, that he really thought I looked worfe than any one in
the boat. The fimplicity with which he uttered fuch an
opinion diverted me, and I had good humour enough to
return him a better compliment.

Every one received his 25th of a pound of bread, and
quarter of a pint of water, at evening, morning, and noon,
and an extra allowance of water was given to thofe who
defired it.

At noon I obferved in latitude 9° 41′ S; courfe S 77° W;
diftance 109 miles; longitude made 13° 49′ W. I had little
doubt of having now paffed the meridian of the eaftern
part of Timor, which is laid down in 128° E. This diffufed
univerfal joy and fatisfaction.

Friday, June the 12th. Frefh breezes and fine weather,
but very hazy. Wind from E to S E.

All the afternoon we had feveral gannets, and many
other birds, about us, that indicated we were near land, and
at fun-fet we kept a very anxious look-out. In the evening we caught a booby, which I referved for our dinner the
next day.

At

At three in the morning, with an excefs of joy, we dif-covered Timor bearing from W S W to W N W, and I hauled on a wind to the N N E till day-light, when the land bore from S W by S about two leagues to N E by N feven leagues.

It is not poffible for me to defcribe the pleafure which the bleffing of the fight of land diffufed among us. It ap-peared fcarce credible, that in an open boat, and fo poorly provided, we fhould have been able to reach the coaft of Timor in forty-one days after leaving Tofoa, having in that time run, by our log, a diftance of 3618 miles, and that, notwithftanding our extreme diftrefs, no one fhould have perifhed in the voyage.

I have already mentioned, that I knew not where the Dutch fettlement was fituated; but I had a faint idea that it was at the S W part of the ifland. I therefore, after day-light, bore away along fhore to the S S W, and the more readily as the wind would not fuffer us to go towards the N E without great lofs of time.

The day gave us a moft agreeable profpect of the land, which was interfperfed with woods and lawns; the interior part mountainous, but the fhore low. Towards noon the coaft became higher, with fome remarkable head-lands. We were greatly delighted with the general look of the country, which exhibited many cultivated fpots and beau-tiful fituations; but we could only fee a few fmall huts, whence I concluded no European refided in this part of the ifland. Much fea ran on the fhore, fo that landing with a boat was impracticable. At noon I was abreaft of a very high head-land; the extremes of the land bore S W ¼ W, and N N E ½ E; our diftance off fhore being three miles; latitude, by obfervation, 9° 59 S; and my longi-

L

tude,

1789
June 12

tude, by dead reckoning, from the north part of New Holland, 15° 6′ W.

With the usual allowance of bread and water for dinner, I divided the bird we had caught the night before, and to the surgeon and Lebogue I gave a little wine.

Saturday
13.

Saturday, June the 13th. Fresh gales at E, and E S E, with very hazy weather.

During the afternoon, we continued our course along a low woody shore, with innumerable palm-trees, called the Fan Palm from the leaf spreading like a fan; but we had now lost all signs of cultivation, and the country had not so fine an appearance as it had to the eastward. This, however, was only a small tract, for by sun-set it improved again, and I saw several great smokes where the inhabitants were clearing and cultivating their grounds. We had now ran 25 miles to the W S W since noon, and were W five miles from a low point, which in the afternoon I imagined had been the southernmost land, and here the coast formed a deep bend, with low land in the bight that appeared like islands. The west shore was high; but from this part of the coast to the high cape which we were abreast of yesterday noon, the shore is low, and I believe shoal. I particularly remark this situation, because here the very high ridge of mountains, that run from the east end of the island, terminate, and the appearance of the country suddenly changes for the worse, as if it was not the same island in any respect.

That we might not run past any settlement in the night, I determined to preserve my station till the morning, and therefore hove to under a close-reefed fore-sail, with which the boat lay very quiet. We were here in shoal water, our distance from the shore being half a

league,

league, the westernmost land in sight bearing **W S W ¼ W**. Served bread and water for supper, and the boat lying too very well, all but the officer of the watch endeavoured to get a little sleep.

At two in the morning, we wore, and stood in shore till day-light, when I found we had drifted, during the night, about three leagues to the **W S W**, the southernmost land in sight bearing W. On examining the coast, and not seeing any sign of a settlement, we bore away to the westward, having a strong gale, against a weather current, which occasioned much sea. The shore was high and covered with wood, but we did not run far before low land again formed the coast, the points of which opening at west, I once more fancied we were on the south part of the island; but at ten o'clock we found the coast again inclining towards the south, part of it bearing W S W ¼ W. At the same time high land appeared from S W to S W by W ÷ W; but the weather was so hazy, that it was doubtful whether the two lands were separated, the opening only extending one point of the compass. I, for this reason, stood towards the outer land, and found it to be the island Roti.

I returned to the shore I had left, and in a sandy bay I brought to a grapnel, that I might more conveniently calculate my situation. In this place we saw several smokes, where the natives were clearing their grounds. During the little time we remained here, the master and carpenter very much importuned me to let them go in search of supplies; to which, at length, I assented; but, finding no one willing to be of their party, they did not choose to quit the boat. I stopped here no longer than for the purpose just mentioned, and we continued steering

L 2

along

along fhore. We had a view of a beautiful-looking country, as if formed by art into lawns and parks. The coaft is low, and covered with woods, in which are innumerable fan palm-trees, that look like cocoa-nut walks. The interior part is high land, but very different from the more eaftern parts of the ifland, where it is exceedingly mountainous, and to appearance the foil better.

At noon, the ifland Roti bore S W by W feven leagues. I had no obfervation for the latitude, but, by account, we were in 10° 12′ S; our courfe fince yefterday noon being S 77 W, 54 miles. The ufual allowance of bread and water was ferved for breakfaft and dinner, and to the furgeon and Lebogue, I gave a little wine.

Sunday, June the 14th. A ftrong gale at E S E, with hazy weather, all the afternoon; after which the wind became moderate.

At two o'clock this afternoon, having run through a very dangerous breaking fea, the caufe of which I atributed to a ftrong tide fetting to windward, and fhoal water, we difcovered a fpacious bay or found, with a fair entrance about two or three miles wide. I now conceived hopes that our voyage was nearly at an end, as no place could appear more eligible for fhipping, or more likely to be chofen for an European fettlement: I therefore came to a grapnel near the eaft fide of the entrance, in a fmall fandy bay, where we faw a hut, a dog, and fome cattle; and I immediately fent the boatfwain and gunner away to the hut, to difcover the inhabitants.

The S W point of the entrance bore W ½ S three miles; the S E point S by W three quarters of a mile; and the ifland Roti from S by W ¾ W to S W ¼ W, about five leagues.

5   While

While we lay here I found the ebb came from the northward, and before our departure the falling of the tide difcovered to us a reef of rocks, about two cables length from the fhore; the whole being covered at high-water, renders it dangerous. On the oppofite fhore alfo appeared very high breakers; but there is neverthelefs plenty of room, and certainly a fafe channel for a firft-rate man of war. 1789.
JUNE 14.

The bay or found within, feemed to be of a confiderable extent; the northern part, which I had now in view, being about five leagues diftant. Here the land made in moderate rifings joined by lower grounds. But the ifland Roti, which lies to the fouthward, is the beft mark to know this place.

I had juft time to make thefe remarks, when I faw the boatfwain and gunner returning with fome of the natives: I therefore no longer doubted of our fuccefs, and that our moft fanguine expectations would be fully gratified. They brought five Indians, and informed me that they had found two families, where the women treated them with European politenefs. From thefe people I learned, that the governor refided at a place called Coupang, which was fome diftance to the N E. I made figns for one of them to go in the boat, and fhow me Coupang, intimating that I would pay him for his trouble; the man readily complied, and came into the boat.

Thefe people were of a dark tawny colour, and had long black hair; they chewed a great deal of beetle, and wore a fquare piece of cloth round their hips, in the folds of which was ftuck a large knife. They had a handkerchief wrapped round their heads, and at their fhoulders hung

another

another tied by the four corners, which served as a bag for their beetle equipage.

They brought us a few pieces of dried turtle, and some ears of Indian corn. This last was most welcome to us; for the turtle was so hard, that it could not be eaten without being first soaked in hot water. Had I staid they would have brought us something more; but, as the pilot was willing, I was determined to push on. It was about half an hour past four when we sailed.

By direction of the pilot we kept close to the east shore under all our sail; but as night came on, the wind died away, and we were obliged to try at the oars, which I was surprised to see we could use with some effect. However, at ten o'clock, as I found we got but little ahead, I came to a grapnel, and for the first time I issued double allowance of bread and a little wine to each person.

At one o'clock in the morning, after the most happy and sweet sleep that ever men had, we weighed, and continued to keep the east shore on board, in very smooth water; when at last I found we were again open to the sea, the whole of the land to the westward, that we had passed, being an island, which the pilot called Pulo Samow. The northern entrance of this channel is about a mile and a half or two miles wide, and I had no ground at ten fathoms.

Hearing the report of two cannon that were fired, gave new life to every one; and soon after we discovered two square-rigged vessels and a cutter at anchor to the eastward. I endeavoured to work to windward, but we were obliged to take to our oars again, having lost ground on each tack. We kept close to the shore, and continued rowing till four o'clock, when I brought to a grapnel, and gave another allowance of bread and wine to

4

all

all hands. As foon as we had refted a little, we weighed
again, and rowed till near day-light, when I came to a grapnel, off a fmall fort and town, which the pilot told me was Coupang.

Among the things which the boatfwain had thrown into the boat before we left the fhip, was a bundle of fignal flags that had been made for the boats to fhow the depth of water in founding; with thefe I had, in the courfe of the paffage, made a fmall jack, which I now hoifted in the main fhrouds, as a fignal of diftrefs; for I did not choofe to land without leave.

Soon after day-break a foldier hailed me to land, which I inftantly did, among a croud of Indians, and was agreeably furprifed to meet with an Englifh failor, who belonged to one of the veffels in the road. His captain, he told me, was the fecond perfon in the town; I therefore defired to be conducted to him, as I was informed the governor was ill, and could not then be fpoken with.

Captain Spikerman received me with great humanity. I informed him of our miferable fituation; and requefted that care might be taken of thofe who were with me, without delay. On which he gave directions for their immediate reception at his own houfe, and went himfelf to the governor, to know at what time I could be permitted to fee him; which was fixed to be at eleven o'clock.

I now defired every one to come on fhore, which was as much as fome of them could do, being fcarce able to walk: they, however, got at laft to the houfe, and found tea with bread and butter provided for their breakfaft.

The abilities of a painter, perhaps, could never have been difplayed to more advantage than in the delineation of the two groups of figures, which at this time prefented
themfelves.

themfelves. An indifferent fpectator would have been at a lofs which moft to admire; the eyes of famine fparkling at immediate relief, or the horror of their piefervers at the fight of fo many fpectres, whofe ghaftly countenances, if the caufe had been unknown, would rather have excited terror than pity. Our bodies were nothing but fkin and bones, our limbs were full of fores, and we were cloathed in rags; in this condition, with the tears of joy and gratitude flowing down our cheeks, the people of Timor beheld us with a mixture of horror, furprife, and pity.

The governor, Mr. William Adrian Van Efte, notwithftanding his extreme ill-health, became fo anxious about us, that I faw him before the appointed time. He received me with great affection, and gave me the fulleft proofs that he was poffeffed of every feeling of a humane and good man. Sorry as he was, he faid, that fuch a calamity could ever have happened to us, yet he confidered it as the greateft bleffing of his life that we had fallen under his protection; and, though his infirmity was fo great that he could not do the office of a friend himfelf, he would give fuch orders as I might be certain would procure me every fupply I wanted. In the mean time a houfe was hired for me, and, till matters could be properly regulated, victuals for every one were ordered to be dreffed at his own houfe. With refpect to my people, he faid I might have room for them either at the hofpital or on board of captain Spikerman's fhip, which lay in the road; and he expreffed much uneafinefs that Coupang could not afford them better accommodations, the houfe affigned to me being the only one uninhabited, and the fituation of the few families fuch, that they could not accommodate any one. After this converfation an elegant repaft was fet before me, more according to the

cuftom

cuftom of the country, than with defign to alleviate my hunger : fo that in this inftance he happily blended, with common politenefs, the greateft favour I could receive.

On returning to my people, I found every kind relief had been given to them. The furgeon had dreffed their fores, and the cleaning of their perfons had not been lefs attended to, befides feveral friendly gifts of apparel.

I now defired to be fhewn to the houfe that was intended for me, and I found it ready, with fervants to attend, and a particular one, which the governor had directed to be always about my perfon. The houfe confifted of a hall, with a room at each end, and a loft over-head; and was furrounded by a piazza, with an outer apartment in one corner, and a communication from the back part of the houfe to the ftreet. I therefore determined, inftead of feparating from my people, to lodge them all with me; and I divided the houfe as follows: One room I took to myfelf, the other I allotted to the mafter, furgeon, Mr. Nelfon, and the gunner; the loft to the other officers; and the outer apartment to the men. The hall was common to the officers, and the men had the back piazza. Of this I informed the governor, and he fent down chairs, tables, and benches, with bedding and other neceffaries for the ufe of every one.

The governor, when I took my leave, had defired me to acquaint him with every thing of which I ftood in need; but I was now informed it was only at particular times that he had a few moments of eafe, or could attend to any thing; being in a dying ftate, with an incurable difeafe. On this account, whatever bufinefs I had to tranfact would be with Mr. Timotheus Wanjon, the fecond of this place, and the governor's fon-in-law; who now alfo was contribut-

ing

ing every thing in his power to make our situation comfortable. I had been, therefore, misinformed by the seaman, who told me that captain Spikerman was the next person to the governor

At noon a very handsome dinner was brought to the house, which was sufficient to make persons, more accustomed to plenty, eat too much. Cautions, therefore, might be supposed to have had little effect; but I believe few people in such a situation would have observed more moderation. My greatest apprehension was, that they would eat too much fruit.

Having seen every one enjoy this meal of plenty, I dined with Mr. Wanjon; but I found no extraordinary inclination to eat or drink. Rest and quiet, I considered, as more necessary to my doing well, and therefore retired to my room, which I found furnished with every convenience. But, instead of rest, my mind was disposed to reflect on our late sufferings, and on the failure of the expedition; but, above all, on the thanks due to Almighty God, who had given us power to support and bear such heavy calamities, and had enabled me at last to be the means of saving eighteen lives.

In times of difficulty there will generally arise circumstances that bear more particularly hard on a commander. In our late situation, it was not the least of my distresses, to be constantly assailed with the melancholy demands of my people for an increase of allowance, which it grieved me to refuse. The necessity of observing the most rigid œconomy in the distribution of our provisions was so evident, that I resisted their solicitations, and never deviated from the agreement we made at setting out. The consequence of this care was, that at our arrival we had still remaining

maining fufficient for eleven days, at our fcanty allowance: and if we had been fo unfortunate as to have miffed the Dutch fettlement at Timor, we could have proceeded to Java, where I was certain every fupply we wanted could be procured.

Another difagreeable circumftance, to which my fituation expofed me, was the caprice of ignorant people. Had I been incapable of acting, they would have carried the boat on fhore as foon as we made the ifland of Timor, without confidering that landing among the natives, at a diftance from the European fettlement, might have been as dangerous as among any other Indians.

The quantity of provifions with which we left the fhip, was not more than we fhould have confumed in five days, had there been no neceffity for hufbanding our ftock. The mutineers muft naturally have concluded that we could have no other place of refuge than the Friendly Iflands; for it was not likely they fhould imagine, that, fo poorly equipped as we were in every refpect, there could have been a poffibility of our attempting to return homewards: much lefs will they fufpect that the account of their villany has already reached their native country.

When I reflect how providentially our lives were faved at Tofoa, by the Indians delaying their attack, and that, with fcarce any thing to fupport life, we croffed a fea of more than 1200 leagues, without fhelter from the inclemency of the weather; when I reflect that in an open boat, with fo much ftormy weather, we efcaped foundering, that not any of us were taken off by difeafe, that we had the great good fortune to pafs the unfriendly natives of other countries without accident, and at laft happily to meet with the moft friendly and beft of people to relieve our dif-

M 2   treffes;

treffes; I fay, when I reflect on all thefe wonderful efcapes, the remembrance of fuch great mercies enables me to bear, with refignation and chearfulnefs, the failure of an expedition, the fuccefs of which I had fo much at heart, and which was fruftrated at a time when I was congratulating myfelf on the faireft profpect of being able to complete it in a manner that would fully have anfwered the intention of his Majefty, and the honourable promoters of fo benevolent a plan.

With refpect to the prefervation of our health, during a courfe of 16 days of heavy and almoft continual rain, I would recommend to every one in a fimilar fituation the method we practifed, which is to dip their cloaths in the falt-water, and wring them out, as often as they become filled with rain; it was the only refource we had, and I believe was of the greateft fervice to us, for it felt more like a change of dry cloaths than could well be imagined. We had occafion to do this fo often, that at length all our cloaths were wrung to pieces: for, except the few days we paffed on the coaft of New Holland, we were continually wet either with rain or fea.

Thus, through the affiftance of Divine Providence, we furmounted the difficulties and diftreffes of a moft perilous voyage, and arrived fafe in an hofpitable port, where every neceffary and comfort were adminiftered to us with a moft liberal hand.

Timor.

As, from the great humanity and attention of the governor, and the gentlemen, at Coupang, we received every kind of affiftance, we were not long without evident figns of returning health: therefore, to fecure my arrival at Batavia, before the October fleet failed for Europe, on the firft of July, I purchafed a fmall fchooner, 34 feet long,

for

for which I gave 1000 rix-dollars, and fitted her for fea, under the name of His Majefty's fchooner Refource.

On the 20th of July, I had the misfortune to lofe Mr. David Nelfon: he died of an inflammatory fever. The lofs of this honeft man I very much lamented: he had accomplifhed, with great care and diligence, the object for which he was fent, and was always ready to forward every plan I propofed, for the good of the fervice we were on. He was equally ufeful in our voyage hither, in the courfe of which he gave me great fatisfaction, by the patience and fortitude with which he conducted himfelf.

July 21ft. This day I was employed attending the funeral of Mr. Nelfon. The corpfe was carried by twelve foldiers dreft in black, preceded by the minifter; next followed myfelf and fecond governor; then ten gentlemen of the town and the officers of the fhips in the harbour; and after them my own officers and people.

After reading our burial-fervice, the body was interred behind the chapel, in the burying-ground appropriated to the Europeans of the town. I was forry I could get no tombftone to place over his remains.

This was the fecond voyage Mr. Nelfon had undertaken to the South Seas, having been fent out by Sir Jofeph Banks, to collect plants, feeds, &c. in Captain Cook's laft voyage. And now, after furmounting fo many difficulties, and in the midft of thankfulnefs for his deliverance, he was called upon to pay the debt of nature, at a time leaft expected.

Auguft the 20th. After taking an affectionate leave of the hofpitable and friendly inhabitants, I embarked, and we failed from Coupang, exchanging falutes with the fort and fhipping as we ran out of the harbour.

I left

1789.
AUGUST.
I left the governor, Mr. Van Efte, at the point of death. To this gentleman our moft grateful thanks are due, for the humane and friendly treatment that we have received from him. His ill ftate of health only prevented him from fhowing us more particular marks of attention. Unhappily, it is to his memory only that I now pay this tribute. It was a fortunate circumftance for us, that Mr. Wanjon, the next in place to the governor, was equally humane and ready to relieve us. His attention was unremitting, and, when there was a doubt about fupplying me with money, on government account, to enable me to purchafe a veffel, he chearfully took it upon himfelf; without which, it was evident, I fhould have been too late at Batavia to have failed for Europe with the October fleet. I can only return fuch fervices by ever retaining a grateful remembrance of them.

Mr. Max, the town furgeon, likewife behaved to us with the moft difinterefted humanity: he attended every one with the utmoft care; for which I could not prevail on him to receive any payment, or to render me any account, or other anfwer, than that it was his duty.

Coupang is fituated in 10° 12′ S latitude, and 124° 41′ E longitude.

Auguft 29

On the 29th of Auguft, I paffed by the weft end of the Ifland Flores, through a dangerous ftrait full of iflands and rocks; and, having got into the latitude of 8° S, I fteered to the weft, paffing the iflands Sumbawa, Lombock, and Bali, towards Java, which I faw on the 6th of September. I continued my courfe to the weft, through the Straits of Madura.

September 10.
Paffourwang.

On the 10th of September, I anchored off Paffourwang, in latitude 7° 36′ S, and 1° 44′ W of Cape Sandana, the N E end of Java.

3

On

On the 11th I failed, and on the 13th arrived at Soura-bya, latitude 7° 11′ S, 1° 52′ weft.

On the 17th of September, failed from Sourabya, and the fame day anchored at Criffey, for about two hours,' and from thence I proceeded to Samarang. Latitude of Criffey 7° 9′ S, 1° 55′ weft.

On the 22d of September, anchored at Samarang; latitude 6° 54′ S, 4° 7′ W. And on the 26th I failed for Batavia, where I arrived on the 1ft of October. Latitude 6° 10′ S; 8° 12′ W from the eaft end of Java.

On the day after my arrival, having gone through fome fatigue in adjufting matters to get my people out of the fchooner, as fhe lay in the river, and in an unhealthy fituation, I was feized with a violent fever.

On the 7th, I was carried into the country, to the phyfician-general's houfe, where, the governor-general informed me, I fhould be accommodated with every attendance and convenience; and to this only can I attri-bute my recovery. It was, however, neceffary for me to quit Batavia without delay; and the governor, on that ac-count, gave me leave, with two others, to go in a packet that was to fail before the fleet; and affured me, that thofe who remained fhould be fent after me by the fleet, which was to fail before the end of the month: that if I remain-ed, which would be highly hazardous, he could not fend us all in one fhip. My failing, therefore, was eligible, even if it had not been neceffary for my health; and for that reafon I embarked in the Vlydt packet, which failed on the 16th of October.

On the 16th of December, I arrived at the Cape of Good Hope, where I firft obferved that my ufual health was returning;

returning; but for a long time I continued very weak and infirm.

I received the greateſt attention and politenefs from the governor-general, and all the reſidents on the coaſt of Java; and particular marks of friendſhip and regard from the governor, M. Van de Graaf, at the Cape of Good Hope.

On the 2d of January, 1790, we failed for Europe, and on the 14th of March, I was landed at Portfmouth by an Iſle of Wight boat.

F   I   N   I   S.

Lightning Source UK Ltd.
Milton Keynes UK
UKOW04f0054110417

298805UK00001B/27/P

9 781170 397008